Paradoxes of Peace

Library of Congress Cataloging-in-Publication Data

Mosley, Nicholas, 1923-
  Paradoxes of peace, or, The presence of infinity / by Nicholas Mosley.
    p. cm.
  ISBN 978-1-56478-539-8 (pbk. : acid-free paper)
  1. Mosley, Nicholas, 1923- 2. Mosley, Nicholas, 1923---Religion. 3.
Mosley, Nicholas, 1923---Political and social views. 4. Mosley, Oswald,
1896-1980--Political and social views. 5. Authors, English--20th century--Bi-
ography. 6. Biographers--Great Britain--Biography. 7. Editors--Great Britain-
-Biography. I. Title. II. Title: Paradoxes of peace. III. Title: Presence of infinity.
  PR6063.O82Z466 2009
  823'.914--dc22
  [B]
                              2008046919

Partially funded by a grant from the Illinois Arts Council, a state agency, and
by the University of Illinois at Urbana-Champaign

www.dalkeyarchive.com
Cover: design by Danielle Dutton, illustration by Nicholas Motte
Printed on permanent/durable acid-free paper and bound in the
United States of America

Paradoxes of Peace
or The Presence of Infinity

Nicholas Mosley

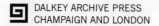
DALKEY ARCHIVE PRESS
CHAMPAIGN AND LONDON

Humans seem at home in war. They feel lost when among the respon-
sibilities of peace. In war they are told what to do; they accept that they
have to 'get on with it.' In peace it seems uncertain what they have to do;
they have to discover what the 'it' is to get on with.

This was the start of the last chapter of my memoir *Time at War*,
describing my arrival back in England in September 1945, having spent
two years as an infantry officer fighting from North Africa up through
Italy and into Austria. The war in Europe ended in May 1945, but there
was still the war against Japan; and I was young enough to be of the
age-group designated to go to the Far East. First however we were to be
given a month's leave at home, so I travelled from Austria back down
Italy to Naples, and there waited with a group of friends for the boat
to take us to England. We were sitting on the terrace of the Officers'
Club one evening looking out across the beautiful bay when the news
came through of the dropping of an atomic bomb on Hiroshima; and
then a few days later there were reports of the surrender of Japan. It
would have been impossible for me not to be elated by this news; I was
exhausted by war, and how many more horrific years might there have
been before we could occupy Japan? But now – what on earth was this

miraculous 'atom' bomb: something to do with the force that both held together and exploded the stuff at the heart of matter? Quite God-like indeed! But still, my friends and I would presumably still have to go off for some wearisome mopping-up operations in the Far East.

Then when I got home to London in September 1945 I found that the whole grandiose social whirl had started up again, as if there had been only a blip since September 1939. Almost every night there were what used to be known as debutante dances, to which those considered acceptable were invited and to which I had the entree through my sister Vivien and my aunt Irene Ravensdale. And each of these dances seemed to consist of an enchanted garden of girls. How was it that I had taken so little note of girls before? At public school and then as an army recruit (reputedly dosed with bromide in our tea) – well, perhaps this was understandable. And then in Italy there had been such dire and extravagant warnings about the likely effects of going with local women – including illustrations of physical deformities attendant on syphilis and gonorrhoea – that this had made it all too easy to cling to virginity. But now in London I wanted to collect great armfuls of these available girls; but with them too it seemed there were taboos.

It was thought not proper to 'proposition' more than one girl at a time; and to 'go the whole hog' (as the phrase then was) landed one with expectations of marriage. And yet the force of one's desire indiscriminately to 'gather ye rosebuds ye may' seemed to have the explosive strength of whatever it was at the heart of matter. This was a first paradox of peace – the strings of sexuality and social customs seemed to tie one into knots. And there I had only a week or two before the boat left for Japan!

But might a paradox produce not only desolation, but also another miracle?

One evening, at a dance in a grand London hotel teeming with allurement, I retired to the bar to gain a respite from my fevered efforts to chat up, or to gather up, half a dozen girls at once, and there I came across a major I knew slightly, or perhaps he was a friend of my sisters, and he asked me what I was doing nowadays, and I said I was just off to the Far East. And he said 'My dear fellow, why do you want to do that?' And I said 'I don't.' So he said 'Come and see me in the War Office in the morning.' So I did, and I did not know if he would even remember me. But there he was behind his desk, and he said 'I'm afraid I can't quite manage the War Office, but would a job in Eastern Command, Hounslow, do?' And I said 'Indeed, thank you, Eastern Command, Hounslow, would do very well!' And so in a day or two I received papers taking me off the draft to the Far East and telling me to report to Hounslow Barracks, a gaunt building like a furniture depository, but only forty minutes by underground from Central London where I could lodge with my grandmother or aunt, and continue my juvenile researches into the natural history of girls.

But then, as soon as time-pressure was lifted, there was the problem of how on earth, amongst such profusion, one might be led to pick just one particular girl rather than another? Sexual desire? Companionship? Social compatibility? But since it seemed that a lifetime might be at stake, surely something more outlandish, even mystical, was required: some jungle-test that animals make use of like a smell?

There was a girl I had taken special note of at one of the London dances and I thought she had taken note of me; but I had not pursued her or pounced – for would not the natural outcome of a pounce be to drive a worthy quarry away? But then I came across this girl a week or two later in a coffee-bar in Oxford, and I asked her if she remembered me, and she said 'Oh yes, I thought you were that murderer.' There was a notorious murderer on the loose at the time who chopped women up and dissolved them in the bath. Well, this could be said to be out-landish! And then when we were having dinner the next day (a suspect murderer might surely be expected to pounce) she was silent for a time while I rattled on, and then when I stopped in order to ask her what she was thinking, she said – 'That I could send you mad in a fortnight.' So – so – some jungle-testing indeed! Anyway, whatever it was, I seemed to be finding it irresistible.

I have told the story of these my first meetings with my future first wife Rosemary at the end of *Time at War*, and there is no need to go into many of the somewhat crazy details again. But the point was – I was evidently in a fairly crazy condition myself on return from war, and needed someone to hold on to who might be compatible with my confusion. My first heartfelt love on my return from Italy had been for a girl (I am going to continue to use the now-unfashionable word 'girl' because this was the heartfelt word at the time) who was both very pretty and yet practical and hardworking, and thus in these ways might seem to be complementary to me. But after a time we both came to feel that my vagaries might tip one or both of us over the edge. Rosemary, whom I met when my first love had gone to work as a secretary at the inaugural United Nations meetings in New York, was someone who seemed to be in tune with my feeling that it was the world that was half over the edge, but that she and I together might be able to hang on by our fingertips.

It is only in my old age that I have been able to see in what an almost clinically unstable condition I must have been at the end of the war. Nowadays it seems to be accepted that people who have experienced war may need 'counselling.' I had gone straight from school into the army when I was eighteen and for a year and a half had been engaged on and off in traumatic fighting. And before this, oh yes (oh dear!), my mother had died when I was nine, reputedly of a broken heart, and my father had gone to prison when I was sixteen; he had been the leader of the British Union of Fascists, and in war was seen as a security risk. None of this had struck me at the time as a reason for myself to be particularly disturbed – indeed I had looked on my war-time relationship with my father as one of the things that had kept me comparatively sane – we had talked and then corresponded lengthily about ideas, books, philosophy – anything but politics. But now, in 1946 here I was finding it difficult to get out of bed in the morning to go to Hounslow to do my boring job which concerned officers' pay and courts-martial; and difficult to get through the day in any reasonable condition until I could start drinking in the evenings.

At this time I still had a bad stammer that had started in childhood (how I had been accepted as an army officer I do not know, except that at times of life-or-death crises stammerers may become articulate). But much of my job in Hounslow depended on the telephone, and this was a torment; and my ability to partake in any social life in the evenings came to depend more and more on alcohol. The army did in fact after the war arrange most helpfully for me to have 'counselling' for my stammer. I was sent to one of the few speech specialists who ever seemed to me to make sense. He told me – 'A stammer can be a defence-mechanism against other people's potential aggression against oneself; but also, and perhaps more importantly, it can be a curb on the stammerer's feelings of aggression against other people.' Much of my early sense of being at odds with the world had taken the form of thinking it was the world that was mad rather than myself; and perhaps I needed to be protected from too often expressing this too.

Also – Hence the need to find someone I loved who would feel her-

self sufficiently an 'outsider' not to need to get carried off in the main-
stream of society, but not such a 'loner' as to be swept with me towards
any available shallows or rapids.

When I first started taking Rosemary out in Oxford – she was at the
Ruskin School of Art; I had got out of the army a year early in October
1946 to take up a place being kept for me at Balliol – after our first eccentric meetings I had got the impression that she must come from a
poor if unusual family, because in spite of her appearance at a debutante
ball she now wore somewhat dilapidated clothes and did not seem to
have enough money for bus fares. For our third meeting I suggested
that the following Sunday we might go for a drive in my car, and she
said could we go and visit her old grandmother in Hertfordshire. I said
– Indeed – and was interested to see (though such was the style of our
budding relationship that I did not think it would be a good tactic to
inquire) what I would find.

So on Sunday we drove through country lanes and came eventually
to the gates and lodge of what seemed to be a drive that would lead to
a large country house. An old lady came out from the lodge to open
the gates. I wondered – Is this Rosemary's grandmother? The old lady
waved us through. We drove across what seemed to be endless acres
of parkland and came to a long low house like a battleship. We went
in through a back door and along stone passages where all life seemed
to have stopped; then through a green baize door. We paused outside
what might be a small sitting room. Here Rosemary asked me to wait
for a moment. Then when she ushered me in there was a very old lady
in a wheelchair who, when her granddaughter had introduced me, said
'And I was such a friend of your grandfather's!'

I still did not know who this lady was, who had been a friend of
my grandfather George Curzon. (Later that day I managed to catch a

glimpse of an envelope on a desk addressed to 'Lady Desborough.') After some chat she asked Rosemary if I would like to see what she called 'the paintings.' She handed to Rosemary a huge old-fashioned key and we went down a long corridor of tattered grandeur and into a large high picture gallery where, when Rosemary had opened a creaking shutter or two, there appeared – looming through cobwebs – a Van Dyck? A Teniers? A renaissance Holy Family? There was a huge portrait of a soldier on horseback that could be – surely could not be! – a Rembrandt? Rosemary said 'Well, they say it is.' I felt it crucial that I should not appear to be bowled over by all this. Why should not this particular set of circumstances, after all, be as natural as any other? But it did now seem (such indeed is human nature) that there were practical as well as outlandish reasons why we should marry.

Lord Curzon had been my mother's father, viceroy of India, foreign secretary under Lloyd George, then tipped to be prime minister but had had to make way for Baldwin. During my childhood my mother's family had been a counter-weight to my father's disreputable politics. And it seemed there were similar balancing paradoxes here.

Rosemary wanted to be a painter. And although her family (as I was now learning) had in the past been remarkable patrons and collectors of art, it had not seemed easy for Rosemary to break away from the grand style of her background in order to dedicate herself to being an artist. For this not to be too laborious, might not she need to find a partner who also had a foot as it were in both camps?

And indeed I at this time was beginning to need to get away from my father. And I was wanting most urgently, after the postponements of war, to begin to write my first novel.

So did it not seem in the nature of things that we should marry?

When I had been in Italy I had seen little beyond re-establishing a home with my father after the war; and this for a year or so I did, spending weekends with him in Wiltshire both when I was still in the army in Hounslow, and then when I had been demobilised early to take up the place at Balliol. My sister and brother and their entourage either might or might not join my father in Wiltshire. Before the war they had remained in my mother's old home at Denham, in Buckinghamshire, under the care of my aunt Irene, my mother's sister, while my father moved with my stepmother to Derbyshire and I in my school holidays moved between one home and the other. Then both homes had been relinquished, as a consequence of war.

Now, in 1946, at weekends in Wiltshire, my relationship with my father at first worked well. We recaptured the style we had discovered in my visits to prison and then in letters during the war – discussing ideas, books, philosophy. He was out of politics and said he was not going back; from now on he would remain a gentleman farmer, and write. In the autumn of 1945 all the family had gathered to get the harvest in; then in the winter there was pheasant and partridge shooting and in the evenings good food and good wine and good talk. At the same time of course I was being tugged to and fro by my girl or girls in London and Oxford, and before long my father was being tugged back into politics.

Before the war I had not seen much of his political activities; he had arranged that his children should be kept apart. I knew of course that he was the leader of the British Union of Fascists, but we never saw a black shirt at home. I knew that he had come to be known as an anti-Semite, which seemed to me absurd and wrong, though again there had been no talk of this at home. In the summer holidays of 1938 I had argued with Diana about her friendship with Hitler, and she had listened patiently, and said that she hoped that one day if there wasn't a war she might take me to meet him. I had been taken to one of my father's outdoor meetings in Hyde Park in 1934, but nothing could be heard of his speech because of the clatter of a police autogyro overhead. Then in 1938 I went to a packed indoor meeting at Earls Court, the theme of which was the urgent necessity of preventing a Second World War; and with this I could have sympathy. I had some doubts about the war until I joined the army; but then, to be sure, one just had to 'get on with it.' And then my father showed no bitterness about being locked up as a security risk in 1940, because this was evidence of his hostility to war. But he was pleased about myself going off to fight, because this might be evidence of his patriotism.

By 1946 however enough had come out about the horrors of Nazism to end any lingering doubts about the war's necessity, and to make conversations with my father liable to be more difficult. And then by 1947 some of his old followers – though now with blackshirts taboo – had begun to hold meetings in London's East End once more. And although my father stayed away from these for a time, I could see him being lured back, like an old addict, to the excitement of bellowing speeches again from the top of a loudspeaker van.

It was from this that I felt I had to get away. And by the end of 1947 Rosemary and I were married, with the blessing of both our families. And then we were off on a long honeymoon in the West Indies, leaving behind both our families and Oxford – me to be a writer, Rosemary a painter. By great good fortune I had had a sufficient income from a Trust established by my mother's family in America. And after our honeymoon – what? But why, in freedom, should there be any thought of 'after'?

In the West Indies we stayed for a fortnight in Jamaica at a grand hotel in Montego Bay. Here we were spotted by Lord Beaverbrook who asked us out to dinner (who were these two rather spooky rich kids?). And he there told us with relish 'Do you realise that it was *your* grandmother (pointing to Rosemary) who prevented *your* grandfather (pointing to me) from becoming Prime Minister?' His story was that in 1923 Rosemary's grandmother, Ettie Desborough, had had a quiet word in the ear of Arthur Balfour, the conservative party's elder statesman, who had passed on the quiet word to the King; that my grandfather George Curzon ('*such* a friend!') was much too authoritarian and out of touch to be prime minister; and so the job had gone to the somewhat colourless Stanley Baldwin. Neither Rosemary nor I showed much surprise or interest in this. We were not asked to dinner again.

From Jamaica we went island-hopping by plane down to St Lucia, where we found a small island just off the coast called Pigeon Island, which was inhabited only by an eccentric English lady called Mrs Snowball, the local fisherman thinking the island was haunted and refusing to stay there at night. We made friends with Mrs Snowball, and she let us stay in her beach-hut, where I could write and from which Rosemary could go out each day to paint the rocky landscape and the sea and the ruins of an eighteenth-century fort where there was said to lurk the ghost of Admiral Romney. And in the evenings we could share with Mrs Snowball the meal that her servants had left for her before they fled from the island, and listen with her to the news on her radio from the outside world.

This prospect had sounded to us like a rediscovery of the Garden of Eden, and perhaps it was, but how on earth would humans get on back in Eden? Might not one of the reasons that they fell out with God be just that there was no challenge, no involvement?

Rosemary went out to paint each day with not much hope of bumping into Admiral Romney. I began my first novel about a young man returning from the Second World War so traumatised that in spite of his good fortune in loving and being loved by two women at once, he could not settle with either and seemed to get himself rather lazily killed. Why? Because in peace it was too difficult to make choices?

And indeed, in the evenings when Rosemary and I listened to Mrs Snowball's crackling short-wave radio we heard of the world wandering towards another world war only three years after the last. This was the spring of 1948, and there was news of the blockade of West Berlin by the Russians, the airlift by the Allies, suggestions by pundits that America should drop its atom bombs on Russia now before the Russians got theirs, reports that German ex-Nazis who had been imprisoned for atrocities were now being released and reinstated in positions of authority so that they could join in the fight against communism. So all right, Pigeon Island was like Eden, yes; but was it not in the nature of humans to be involved in battles between good and evil, if they could not make up their minds what good and evil were?

Rosemary and I thought of settling on Pigeon Island. But what was the point of writing or painting if it was not to distil some sort of imagination of Eden from the experience of its loss; the image of it seeming to live in human consciousness as something not to be attained but searched for – this being valid only if it was known it could not be attained. So Rosemary and I decided to move on.

And oh yes, I might just be in time to catch the English versus West Indies test-match in Trinidad.

When we were back in England in the summer of 1948 Rosemary and I looked for somewhere to live where we might have one foot on the rim of the politically apparently mad world, and try to find sanity through what we might create. We looked for a property in North Wales, where Rosemary had been happy as an evacuee during the war, and which did seem, when she took me to visit it, poised between wildness and tranquillity. With the money I had saved during the war from the income from my mother's family trust in America (I could not touch the capital) Rosemary and I now bought a small hill farm near Lake Bala in what was then Merionethshire. Here we planned to make our own garden outside Eden, and to work – me to get on with my novel and to run the farm, Rosemary to paint and make curtains and chair-covers and so on. So-called artists should have one foot on the earth, should they not? So that their heads should not float too far into the clouds.

These were words, intentions. But the great outside world did seem to be settling onto some knife-edge balance of hostility – the Communist East depending on its antagonism to the Capitalist West for the maintenance of its own sense of meaning and cohesion, and the West depending on the threat from the East as a means of healing its old wounds and divisions. But what might a newly-married couple be threatened by to encourage cohesion? Poverty, yes; the struggle to make ends meet in building a home. But if such threats were not pressing – then what about embarking on running a hill farm in North Wales with no previous experience of farming except that of helping to bring the harvest in on one's father's estate in Wiltshire, and at the same time writing a first novel of romantic gloom and doom? Well this was supposed to be a challenge, wasn't it, rather than to make sense?

The farm was in wild rolling hills with a stream running past the back door from which one leaned with a bucket to draw water. The source of the stream was high in the hills to which one could walk in a silence and loneliness that seemed almost palpable. A few yards downstream from the farmhouse was a two-seater privy constructed precariously over the stream where one could sit and ruminate and not think too much about the people who might be drawing their water from further down. From the previous owner I had inherited sheep and cows; we added chickens and two geese and a pig. But one had been warned in the myth, had one not, that life outside Eden would not be straightforward.

It rained so much that our sheep wandered off and got their heads stuck in wire; the vet said they were suffering from water on the brain. Our chickens roosted in the trees and their eggs were apt to splash to the ground like hail. After the time had come for one of the geese to be killed, its surviving partner came and stood outside the window of the room in which I was writing my gloom-and-doom novel and honked mournfully at its own reflection in the glass. When the time came for the pig to be killed, the slaughterer came up from the village and I held the pig in my arms while its throat was cut and its life ran out, and it looked up at me reproachfully as if I were that Old Testament God. I thought – Well perhaps things are tough for God, too, yes, if there has to be killing and dying for sustenance, for evolution.

Our farm might be some representation of the great big world as if seen through the wrong end of a telescope, but there were times when, even with my feet as it were on the ground, my head felt not so much in the clouds as like an astronaut lost in space without a lifeline.

Then Rosemary became pregnant. And now in winter snow blocked our mountain roads, and the stream from which we drew our water froze, and the doctor who came to examine Rosemary had nowhere to wash his hands. So where might it be proper to be pregnant – in the cities of the plain? With all modern amenities and corruptions?

It had been part of the original myth that humans should bring forth in pain; but what was responsible pain and what was not? And Rosemary could not now easily paint. And what was I doing writing about death and tragedy?

We had wanted to create. Well, was not pregnancy an ineluctable form of creation?

So we left the farm for two months in the summer, putting it in the care of our farm worker who anyway knew more about the business than I. We rented a small house in London so that the baby could be given a conventional hospital birth. And I found I was quite looking forward to being again amongst our old circle of friends in a city of the plain.

Rosemary gave birth in King's College Hospital, Denmark Hill. There she was kept for a fortnight which was the custom in those days. There were strict and limited visiting hours even for fathers, so I spent the time when I was not at the hospital or driving to and fro, in making with a group of friends and a small 16 mm cine-camera, a home-movie called *The Policeman's Mother*. This was based on a would-be Freudian idea that the strict disciplinary attitudes of people like policemen (or matrons and nurses?) might originate from a frustrated love for their mothers. In the hospital neither Rosemary nor I were allowed to spend much time even holding our baby. I tried not to burden Rosemary with details of my film about cities of the plain.

When Rosemary emerged from the hospital she was still being told by pundits including her mother that a girl from her background could of course not be expected to look after her so-young baby, and certainly not in a place which still had no running water. Thus she should not go back to the farm; she should go with the baby and a trained nurse to stay as long as necessary in her grandmother's vast house in Hertford-shire. And yes, if she wished (like this she would not be in the way of the nurse) she could go during the week to an art school in London. And I could go back to run the farm and indeed – why not? – begin my sec-ond novel without causing or being a prey to distraction. And oh yes, I could see to the installation of the at last promised piped water.

Rosemary and I accepted all this because such were the customs of the time; and it was true that we knew almost as little about babies as I had done about farming. Also, I suppose there was the satisfaction of being able to get on with what we had thought it was proper for us to do, which was paint and write, even if these happened to be blessed by conventions.

We did in fact for a time the next spring all of us squeeze into the farmhouse – Rosemary and I and the baby and a helper who had been the wife of Rosemary's grandmother's chauffeur. And for a time this was all quite jolly. And we did achieve piped water.

But then Rosemary got pregnant again, and nearly had a miscarriage, and the local doctor still seemed not quite to be in touch with washing his hands. So – so – this time Rosemary's family made a determined move to dislodge us from Wales, and her mother offered to hand over to us her commodious house in Sussex which was now too big for her, and in which she hoped that we might more decorously bring up our growing family. And because of what seemed to be the inevitability of the way things were working out – which included my feeling less and less at home in farming – this struck us as an offer we could not refuse.

So after another brief spell in London to attend to another hospital birth, Rosemary with her two baby boys moved to Sussex, and I went back for a time in Wales to pack up our lovely farmhouse. This I did without too much sorrow. Our life there, however often idyllic, had remained like trying to make use of the beauties of outer space.

Things would be less of a worry in Sussex. And we would have a lifeline to the city of the plain.

At roughly the same time as Rosemary became pregnant with our first child, who was christened Shaun, another event had impinged on my life which was to have lasting consequences. This was that my old school-friend Anthony, he who as I have described in *Time at War* sailed with me in 1943 in the troopship to North Africa and later spent time with me in Naples, wrote to me now to say that his experience of post-war vacuity and futility was such that he was thinking of becoming a monk. The style of our friendship at school and in the army had been one of irreverence; this latest twist now seemed to me to be an almost unintelligible surrender – as I suppose Anthony himself might have put it, though with different import.

I wrote to him to say that I thought he had gone mad. He replied that he had met a holy man, Father Raynes, Superior of the Anglican Community of the Resurrection, who had convinced him that there was a system of truth beyond helplessness and vacancy. To become aware of this however was a matter not for words but of experience; words had to be tested. Anthony asked me not to write him off as mad before I had met this Father Raynes; and such a meeting could be arranged without too much difficulty because he, Raynes, was in the course of giving talks on Christianity to the unconvinced which took place at weekends in a country house in Surrey, and one of these was due to take place quite soon. I agreed to attend this weekend together with Rosemary, if only out of loyalty to my oldest friend. But I did not think I would have much difficulty in stumping this Father Raynes with my age-old and well-honed questions.

My objections to Christianity were conventional: how could a loving and all-powerful God allow the innocent to suffer, and so on. Also the whole Garden of Eden story was outrageous: an omniscient God must have set up Adam and Eve to what was called 'sin,' and then had subjected them without appeal to inhumanly vindictive punishment – as far as it was known for ever. His later effort at mitigation was to send his own Son down from heaven to suffer as much as humans. This seemed to me worse than insanity.

But my own feelings of futility were increasing at this time. There were once more days when I felt so depressed that it was almost impossible to get out of bed. It was all very well to be resolute in the face of absurdity and nothingness, but what should happen then? It seemed to be true that religion might give one a sense of purpose and instruction, but what if this was illusion? I had been through all this in my wartime letters to my aunt and to my father. And indeed, in history, religion seemed so often to have been a means of flopping or striding into war – an excuse for people of one predilection self-righteously to assault and torture those of another. In comparison, how little was the evidence for religion as a framework for tolerance and peace!

It was in this state of mind that I went to the house in Surrey to confront Father Raynes. There were some twenty people come to listen to him. I did not feel at ease with the people who ran the weekend; they seemed pleased with themselves in a way that, priggishly, I thought inappropriate for Christians. But I was impressed with Raynes himself. He was tall and gaunt with a shaven head, and in his black robe he seemed iconically other-worldly. When giving his talks he spoke carefully and hesitantly, as if once he might have had a stammer. And afterwards I did not stump him with my age-old questions, because he hardly bothered to answer them at all. He just listened; and after a time said – 'Well if you think your life is meaningless, then you'd better get out of it quick.' I was outraged. I thought – And he's a Christian!

On the last afternoon however I was persuaded to have a personal talk with him; and it so happened (our hosts were good at this) that Father Raynes was on his own in the garden. It was a bright spring day; I went out to him. I told him how I had been impressed with his talks, but I would find it difficult to do or to become what he recommended – he had suggested that if one wanted to become a Christian one should go through the motions of Christian practice, and see – I would find this difficult because I found most Christian people so awful. I don't remember him making any reply to this. I had intended to go on about Christians professing to be humble and yet they were always telling others and even God what they or He should and should not do or be. But what in fact I found myself saying under the bright spring sun was – 'I'm not really so awful.' And I think Father Raynes just grunted. But something decisive seemed to have happened, though I could not say just what.

Later I was told – No one chooses to be converted: it either happens or it does not – and secretly. It is the work of the Holy Spirit.

I worked out for myself – What I suppose I meant about being so awful, was to be at the same time both so arrogant and so helpless.

But if one really was ever going to jump into an unknown deep end, would one not need to be given a bit more of a push?

At roughly the same time as these events, in the course of Rosemary and the children settling into Sussex and myself packing up the farmhouse, I was doing a good deal of travelling to and fro between Wales and Sussex which involved passing through London. On occasions when it was convenient to stay there overnight it seemed sensible to take the opportunity to look up, to renew contact with, old friends. There was a girl whom I had known briefly at Oxford before I took up with Rosemary, and she and her story had touched me emotionally and sometimes haunted me. I had not seen her for four or five years; I wondered what had become of her. On one of the evenings when I was stranded in London I found her telephone number in my old address book, and I rang her up and asked her out to dinner.

This girl had not been a typical denizen of the rosebud garden of girls. As a teenager in the war she had been interned with her mother in a Japanese prison camp; she had suffered from deprivation and near-starvation, and her suffering still showed on her surface like a sheen. This gave her natural beauty an uncanny poignancy; she did not need artistry or affectation to appear to be on a borderline between what was natural and what was beyond it. I had taken her to a party at Oxford, and had felt myself affected by her in a way in which it had seemed urgent to offer her love – which anyway was apt to be my custom at parties. But at the end of the party she had made it plain – No, she was not capable of accepting or enjoying any kind of love. So I had not seen her again. And then I had begun going out with Rosemary. But she had stayed as a force in my mind and in my heart.

So some five years later when I was marooned in London, I asked her out to dinner and she said Yes. And she was much the same as she had been, except that there was now some resolution about her as if she might after all have a hand in her fate. And then at the end of a candle-lit dinner, during which there seemed to be something different from what was customary going on off-stage, she said that she did not think that we should see each other again.

I said – But the last time I saw you, you said you could not love. She said – But that was five years ago. I said – And now? She said – Now you are married.

I thought – All right, but there is surely here something going on off-stage.

She said – But you will write to me, won't you? I said – Yes. She said – Or I don't think it will be bearable.

So I went home. This was not long after I had met Father Raynes. When I had said to him that I was not really so awful, I had been recognising, I suppose, that it was not inevitable I should be so helpless. So now what might I do about what might or might not make things bearable? Father Raynes had said – Well act as if you are not helpless, and see.

But by which he had meant, as I understood it – Go through motions recommended by the Church: pray; go to Mass; make your confession. This latter activity in particular would presumably be a sign both of admitting one's helplessness, and yet doing something about it.

But what might I confess? What we had decided now, this girl and I, was surely not wrong, but right?

It was just one's helplessness that one should confess?

I had kept in touch by letter with my old friend Anthony who was now a novice monk at the House of the Resurrection at Mirfield, in Yorkshire. (He was known as Brother Aelred, because there was already a Brother Anthony in the community.) During recent weeks he had been taking on the painstaking task of trying to deal with my age-old questions about the intellectual absurdities and impossibilities of Christianity, which Father Raynes had not felt it his task to deal with in detail. But Aelred's answers boiled down to the same – God does not provide certainty, but the freedom to choose. Yes, if you look at it rationally, Christianity may indeed seem ridiculous: it is when you are moved to experience it that things can click into place.

I now wrote to Aelred to say that I seemed inexplicably to be being driven to make my confession not because I felt I had done wrong, but because I had met someone in relation to whom I felt that we were being led to do right.

Aelred replied – Truly there is no end to the wonder of Him!

So I went off to make my confession – because I felt I had to do something. And if the world seemed dangerously mad, had I not learned once before, in the war, that if one performed an act of faith then this could, against all reason, result in events miraculously seeming to come out all right. On my way to confession this still made little sense. Afterwards, it seemed to have been a jump into the proper deep end of an ocean.

4

One of the aims of this story is to claim that without a sense of God, or of religion, humans have little chance of experiencing a sense of order or meaning apart from their own predilections or addictions. Of course religion itself can be an addiction, and it seems so often nowadays and in history that it is – which is why it can so easily and reasonably be scorned by rationalists. But the chief aim of this story is to claim that a sense of God is neither rational nor an addiction; because the experience it provides is one of being given freedom to choose.

That Christianity – at least the Christianity exemplified by Christ – is not rational, is a fact often not recognized by the faithful, enabling it to be held in contempt by unbelievers; and this is a chief reason why Christians are in such vulnerable disarray today. The existence of God cannot be proved; the nature of God cannot be logically defined; the teaching of Christ is essentially paradoxical. Paradox is a form of words about which opposing interpretations are possible – or perhaps more sensibly no interpretation at all. A viewer, or listener, finds himself in a situation in which he is landed with the authority to make discoveries for himself.

The Christian story, or myth, begins and continues in paradox. There is the story of the Garden of Eden, which had caused me such irritation in the days before my meeting with Father Raynes. But could this not be interpreted as – Of course God's children had by some means to be got to leave the Garden! It is common experience that children when grown up should leave home, however reluctant they are to do so. But a loving father may find it difficult openly to say this, as he may thus appear unloving. In the Garden the children had been told to be obedient so that, presumably, they might be safe. But if they were ever to become responsible both for themselves and for things on earth – which is what according to the story God had in mind for them – they had to discover their own autonomy. And thus by disobeying God when the time came, and by this providing a reason why they should leave the Garden, they would in fact be fulfilling both his wishes and their own proper destiny.

Could this not openly be said? Well no; for the point was that would-be grown-ups have to be using their freedom to discover things for themselves.

Then when God realized that humans on earth, with their freedom now established, were ignoring or disobeying such guidelines as he had left for them – how should he now act as a good parent? Surely neither by washing his hands of them and thus allowing them most likely to come to some terminal grief, nor by taking away the freedom which he had guaranteed them. (Another common dilemma, surely, confronting a good parent!)

Well, you know the story. After the ineffectuality of miraculously delivered commandments, after the nagging of prophets, God chose to demonstrate the style and truth of his paradoxes by appearing on earth in human form himself. So – no more instructions or complaints; but – incarnation, crucifixion, resurrection – though about the exact nature of these one should never quite feel sure. This is the point – the story has to be open to question – to interpretation and understanding by an individual. What is being demonstrated is that freedom to choose cannot be available through certainty, but through the acceptance of paradox.

This way of seeing can of course be called nonsense. But this is once more the point – it is a story in which you either recognize something of your own experience, or you do not.

The parables and recommendations of the Gospels are paradoxical. The shepherd is responsible for his flock, yet he should leave it to go in search of one sheep that has strayed. The prodigal son goes off to have an adventurous life on his own and is rewarded when he returns, yet the other son is reassured that he has done right to stay at home. Above all, Jesus told people not to sin, yet while on earth he seemed to be most at home among sinners – and indeed it was them whom he said he had come to save. The people of whom he seemed most to disapprove were those who said they had no sin. All this led St Paul in his Epistle to the Romans to find himself tied in a rationalist knot; he remonstrated – Then shall we continue in sin so that grace may abound? To which in the Authorised Version he answers himself succinctly – God forbid! But the validity of his question and of the paradox remains. It seems that by the risking of sin, and the admission of this, not only in the narrative but in patterns of life, the heart may be opened so that the transformation of grace may come in.

But this is no mandate to sin! One cannot indeed say – I will sin so that grace may abound. That is the sin of not admitting the sin as sin. So how is the predicament to be understood?

Choices in life are often choices between potential evils. What one chooses will depend on instinct, on how one's instinct has been nurtured, on one's assessment of the situation at the time. So one chooses what seems less likely to entail sin; and then if it does, and one admits this, then still grace may abound.

At the heart of the Bible story there is the understanding that life on earth is such that one cannot avoid sin; what it is within one's power to do is to recognise this and to admit sin when it happens. What makes this possible and effective in the Christian story is the existence and operation of the Holy Spirit.

The Christian doctrine of the Trinity is dismissed as nonsensical by atheists and Jews and Muslims alike. But without it it seems difficult to make sense of how humans are to deal with life.

In Christian understanding – God the Father is the form of God to do with moral law and order; God the Son is the operation of God which requires mercy and forgiveness; and God the Holy Ghost is that which enables humans to tread delicately or decisively between the two. These are not three Gods but three behests of the One. Without this concept there is endless disputation, and no confidence in choice.

Or perhaps in parabolic terms – the Holy Ghost is like a maverick swimming-pool attendant who leads people to a deep end and gives them the chance to jump in; Jesus is the prototype who gives them courage to do so and a belief they will be rescued if they seem to drown; and then the Church will be there to wrap them up and rub them down.

It has been said that Christianity is the religion that wins by losing. If God had not got his children to disobey him in Eden, then they would have had no freedom. If there had been no incarnation and crucifixion, then there could have been no resurrection nor Holy Spirit through which humans could find understanding and assurance in their own minds and hearts.

There was also, yes, the establishing of the Church on earth as a back-up organization as it were for the Holy Spirit. But Jesus founded his

Church on the disciple that he knew would at times deny him; and then the Church, having gained worldly power, indeed seemed to lose spiritual authority; so that people rebelled and went off like the prodigal son. But still, grace might abound. Lose, win, lose, win. The style, in fact, of life.

Grace comes naturally through sin because obedience to law and order is likely to evoke pride, the most obdurate sin. Sin can open the heart and eyes to humility and thus to God. But law is necessary, because without it nothing can be known for what it is – to be sure, not sin.

Whenever some natural or man-made disaster occurs Christians as well as unbelievers are apt to ask – How can God let this happen? But it is central to the Christian story that God has to let such things happen. God has given freedom to humans and to the workings of the world; without this humans would be animals or machinery. The world works scientifically through cause and effect – though physicists say they continue to discover paradoxes at the heart of the universe and of matter. Humans, with their consciousness and self-consciousness, are essentially paradoxical: they experience determinism and freedom at the same time. They feel they have responsibility for the world, yet without some trust beyond cause-and-effect they seem ineffectual. The Christian story is that God through his incarnation has assured humans of his love for them, and by their recognition of this they can learn to be in partnership with Him. But as Christians worked out so painstakingly so many centuries ago – if you try to pin God down in words, then you may lose him; because love is paradoxical.

5

So, after agreeing not to see my ex-prison-camp loved-one again (I shall call her 'Mary,' which was the name I gave her in the novel I began to write at the time), I went to confess not so much a wrong-doing, as the feeling of anxiety and helplessness as a consequence of doing what seemed right. I remember confession as a rather scruffy business like getting down on one's knees to find something that has rolled under a dresser. But why should not this be a pearl of great price? And afterwards there was certainly a sense of liberation. Something had been lost, but what had been found? Because Mary and I had agreed to write letters, this was something to be getting on with.

I don't suppose we either of us knew much about St Paul's tying himself into knots about sin and grace, nor indeed of what might have been his advice to the non-prodigal son who had stayed at home. It turned out, later, that Mary had at least got hold of St Augustine's 'Love, and do as you like.'

So, after some exchange of letters, we agreed that we had made our gesture as it were to God the Father, to propriety; but now what about God the Son? This seemed to be a question unanswerable in letters. So we arranged to meet, after all, on the steps of the National Gallery.

My favourite paintings there representing grace emerging from danger; meaning from what was haphazard; the saying of what cannot be said!

I learned that during the time when we had not been seeing each other Mary had relapsed into her old wartime sickness; she could not eat, she weakened and lay in bed. So was this or was it not a reason for us to see each other again? All that sickness in the Gospels! Had not that been a means for grace?

From the portico of the National Gallery, what a fluttering of pigeons! I don't think we stayed to look at the pictures. The point was to get her to eat; to deal with the sickness, yes.

Mary and I got into a routine in which I would come up from Sussex and see her and we would have a meal, and she became well; then anxiety or respect for right-and-wrong came in and I would go back to my family in Sussex, and she became ill again. (Ah win/lose, lose/win, the endless belt!) (Like the man running underneath the escalator to get the steps from the top to the bottom: this is not absurdity but metaphor.) And then when I returned to her home in Chelsea where she lived with her mother, her mother accepted me because I made her daughter well. I would sit with her while she lay in bed and we would talk and make each other laugh. Nothing wrong with that? No? She did not at first try to stop me going back to my family – so long as it was understood that I would be seeing her again.

I told Rosemary what I was doing. I said that Mary was ill from her experiences in war-time prison-camp, and when I saw her she became better. I said I realised this was dubious stuff, but what else could I do? I had not planned it. Should I not continue until something seemed to be made more clear? I don't think Rosemary was impressed. But she was not the sort of person to try to divert people from getting on with what they felt they had to do; and she could get on with her painting.

I went to talk to Father Raynes. I stayed for a night or two at the austere but oddly busy House of the Resurrection at Mirfield (the austerity was in there being no ornamentation even in the church; the busyness was in the silence beyond which things seemed to be going on elsewhere). I told Father Raynes about Mary. He seemed not to demur when I said that it had been my feeling of helplessness when confronted by her pain that had led me to confession. I had supposed that he might then say – Anyway you must stop seeing her now. But he said – If she would like it, I will try to see her when I am in London. But when I put this to Mary she, who perhaps saw the rigours of paradox more clearly than I, did not wish to see him. I had assured both him and her that I did not want nor intend to endanger my marriage.

I tried to tell this story in my autobiography *Efforts at Truth*. I still do not know just what to make of it or how to convey it. It can seem a sad or foolish story; even, at times, a squalid one. And I am still saying that by such means grace may abound? But this was not what I was saying at the time: rather – What else can I do?

So I continued on and off to sit by her bed; and the better she became the more I knew that one day I would have to leave her even with the intention of not coming back. But this could not be said, because it would encourage her to stay ill. (This is why humanity stays ill – to keep a hold on God's mercy?) (But is this not holding God to ransom? And is not this what non-believers like Nietzsche despise about Christianity?) But also might not what is thus being encouraged by believers be some catastrophe, some super-sin – but for the chance of super-grace? Luther had said 'Sin strongly, but more strongly have faith and rejoice in Christ.'

But in any case – For God's sake stop talking!

And then eventually, during long summer afternoons with me sitting by her bed, we inched closer and closer like caterpillars on a leaf until we did, yes, what is called go to bed. And so – well – thank goodness that's now done! And so, yes, I really must be getting home.

I am telling this story – I say again – because I want its point to be seen not in what could be called the sleaze, where it would be seen in a godless world; but in how things may work out if you are trying to come to some understanding of the paradox-merchants of religion – St Paul, St Augustine, St Julian of Norwich with her mantra 'All shall be well and all manner of things shall be well' – so long, that is, as you have faith.

Mary became well enough for us to go on a motoring-trip to the west-country – as proof as it were of her recovery. We stayed in hotels; we behaved as normal lovers. So this was what life might have been like in another world; and now just for a moment might it not be the best of what was available in this? Because now I could leave her? As before – not because things were bad, because they were good. Not unlike the story of the Gospels? I mean, life has to evolve in stages: one has to be ready for the gift of the Spirit: no?

But indeed, putting this stuff into words is not bearable for long.

Anyway the time came when I told Mary I would be going on a long summer holiday with my wife Rosemary and I was not sure when I would be coming back. I had never given assurance of anything different, had I? (Oh yes, and I had now had my wicked way!) Then I wrote to Mary from Sussex saying I was leaving the next day. She telephoned to say she had to see me. She came by train to our local town and we met in the bar of a hotel.

This was a time when grace seemed to have run out. The escalator or endless belt that had run between the best of both worlds had broken down and seemed beyond repair; and now we had to make our own way up or down. She must see that, mustn't she? Oh it was unbearable, yes, but we had had a good run of the other thing, hadn't we? So how much more lucky can one get! (The language itself becomes tawdry).

And the future? Well, pray, yes. And then in peace, as in war, get on with it.

When I had first told Mary I might be going on a long summer holiday and she had said she did not know if she could bear it, she had asked if I could leave with her something precious to me that she could hold on to. So now in the bar of the hotel I handed to her the Military Cross which I had been awarded in the war, and which had meant as much as anything to me. And she kept this for several years; until the time came when we experienced what was the result of faith, and she could hand it back to me.

So Rosemary and I went off on our holiday, to Spain. We went by car with our great friends, Raymond and Sara Carr; first to Santiago de Compostela, which is where pilgrims used to go when requiring penance. Then down to Avila and Toledo, and back to Pamplona where before bullfights the bulls run through the streets and anyone can run in front of them to show their courage. I saw the point of bullfights, because they were occasions in which there could be demonstrated in a formal way the strange virtue in taking risks. Raymond and I were in the process of climbing over a barricade to run in front of the bulls when our wives, Rosemary and Sara, dragged us back. I was touched by this. I thought – Rosemary might reasonably have been tempted to see me gored.

Once or twice during the goings-on of the previous months Rosemary had called me a deluded fool; but so what, she had believed that I would not break our marriage. And do not men sometimes need to run in front of bulls? And when they come back, it might not be too unlike the return of the prodigal son.

There were times when I wondered what would happen if Mary died; whether this would be what she called bearable. But I had wondered this sort of thing in the war; and had had to get on with it. At places like Santiago de Compostela I suppose I prayed: but prayer was like covering fire; you still had to get on.

And what should I have done differently regarding my loved-one? Never have got in touch with her after the first time at Oxford? Turned my back on her when hurt and danger loomed? Not gone to bed with her? Ah that, yes. But then would grace have had so much of a chance to get on?

When I got back home after some six weeks of holiday I found a letter from Mary's mother saying that her daughter had been extremely ill; and could she, her mother, see me and talk to me? I wrote her a long letter telling the story of her daughter and me as well as I could, and I said that of course I would see her if she still wanted this. But after another letter or two she said she did not. She thanked me for writing so fully, and said her daughter was a little better. One of the brethren from the Community of the Resurrection had been to see her daughter and her; Father Raynes had been away, but he had said he would come when he could. And that might have been that, I suppose, in this potentially humdrum story.

I don't think Father Raynes ever did get to see her. But things went on working themselves out in their own particular way.

A year or so later Father Raynes came to stay with me and Rosemary in our house in Sussex. I had hoped to talk to him about what had happened between me and Mary; that he might offer some judgment or reassurance. But it seemed he was not interested in the past; so why had he come? It was as if he might be concerned about what was happening here and in the present. He sat in our drawing room in his huge black cassock like a figure from another world: he had no small talk; he told stories about when he had been doing battle against apartheid in South Africa. He seemed to show what he might care about in the present when Nanny brought our two sons, aged now three and five, down from the nursery to the drawing-room after tea. This was the customary time for upper-class parents to see their children, before they were taken off again to be put to bed. The children were fascinated by Father Raynes; they hovered around him as he sat ensconced in his chair, they were like animals uncertain about how close to come to an apparition in the jungle. Then he laughed, and the children laughed with him, and they began to touch him as if to see that he was real. He showed them the cross that he wore on a chain round his neck; they leaned on him and seemed to want to climb on him as children or young animals do. Then before he left the next day I asked him if he would tell me anything that had struck him about me and Rosemary – our home, our marriage. He was silent for a moment, as he often was; then he said that he thought Rosemary and I might consider spending more time with our children.

So not long after this we got rid of Nanny – one of whose functions had been, yes, to keep the children for the most part in a separate world. And we began to play games with the children in the afternoons or evenings; we read books to them and put them to bed and said prayers with them. And for ourselves we read works of popular psychology about the bringing up of children – John Bowlby's *Child Care and the Growth of Love*; Ian Suttie's *The Origins of Love and Hate*. And we learned – what? – what most parents nowadays know anyway but which we had not learned from our own parents – that children as they grow are likely to be influenced less by instruction than by the style of their parents' relationship with them; also, and importantly, by their parents' relationship with each other. We continued to employ *au pairs* because it seemed right that Rosemary should have time to paint; and we both continued to hope that this might be part of a valid so-called best of both worlds.

And we hoped that children might learn not only from their parents' style but through their parents' efforts at honesty – however difficult or unseemly might be some of the things their parents were being honest about. Children become aware of family troubles anyway; what they can learn is how these can either be crippling, or not all that important in time if confronted. And it seems to me now that the learning of these lessons was the unequivocal gain of the previous tortuous year.

And could this have been set in train if Father Raynes had not found himself coming to Sussex? And would this have happened if there had not been the risk and then the event of what is commonly called sin – by which was activated the complex pattern of coincidence and interplay through which there might operate what might be called grace? Though this cannot be talked about without the admission of distress and anxiety, no.

And what was happening to Mary during this time? It seemed indeed that in the due order of things this had to remain hidden at least from me. So that there was little I could do but try to learn to pray, and to take part in some of the other exigencies recommended by Father Raynes. Also – oh yes – I would write a novel which would waft a message to my lost loved-one which might assure her of my continued devotion; which might suggest that even if all manner of things did not seem at the moment to be well – they might yet, in the long run, in some form turn out to be.

But this belongs to another chapter of the story.

And in the meantime what other strands of influence might be weaving their touch-and-go patterns?

6

I have told how during the war I had been involved in an intense relationship with my father. Some of my letters to him I printed in my *Time at War*. His letters to me asked if I would return to him after the war because he wanted to make use of the ideas he had expressed in them in the books of *apologia* and manifesto that he now planned to write. In the war I had been nineteen or twenty and was trying to come to terms with the crazy world in which I found myself; my father was in prison and wanting to understand and express how the world was such that he had got into this predicament. We each were in a situation in which it suited us to ruminate. After the war my father did write two books – *My Answer* and *The Alternative*. He had promised to return his letters to me when he had made use of them, but he never did; and by that time we were no longer on such good terms as would have made it easy for me to press him.

He was edging back into politics and I was moving towards writing my first novel, which he thought a low form of literary activity. (He wrote to me 'It is like turning your back on The Derby and entering for the pony races at Northolt' – 'The Derby' presumably being philosophy or history or political analysis, whatever 'the pony races at Northolt' might be.) But we continued to have a common interest in the matter of the pursuit of women – difficult but not impossible for a father and son to talk about. There was a time when my tendency to 'play the field' (my father's term was 'flushing the covers' – a reference to partridge shooting) gave us something to touch on, and my father once showed concern that I did not seem to be going to bed with the girls that I dallied with. Did I not think that this might be unhealthy? But before long I was married and had two children, and my father was back in politics. But still, if the subject arose, there were still some things we could laugh or tease about.

I do not know whether, or when, he knew of my tortuous relationship with Mary, or indeed of my involvement with Father Raynes. But doubtless there was family gossip at least about the latter. And my father enjoyed gossip, so long as it could be turned into jokes. So around this time I had a letter from him – Rosemary and I had been on good enough terms with him and Diana to spend an enjoyable week or two with them in the summer in the south of France – an amused and typical letter, which said –

> I defend you triumphantly against the charge of hypocrisy by saying that you have left Orwell's double-think far behind with a great new scheme of double-fun. We have only the fun of sinning. You have also the fun of repenting.

And later –

> Don't go and cut off the offending member or some other masochistic Protestant trick. I so much prefer the Catholic sense that a healthy lapse can bring you nearer to a state of grace.

I thought – So my father knows about grace, does he?

He would not of course have disapproved of any continued dalliance in the bluebell woods of girls whether I was married or not. But he would, indeed, feel more put out by my contacts with Christianity. For although in his wartime letters he had seen the point of Christianity as exemplified in the Gospels, I would have expected any profession of allegiance to a dogmatic Church to call forth a Nietzschean anathema. However in fact he was soon jokingly referring to himself as Father Sunshine in contrast to Father Raynes (Raynes = Rains, get it?).

And so such letters as he wrote to me now were of guarded encouragement rather than disapproval. Regarding sexual shenanigans (including his own?) his instinct had always been to laugh, to tease. And indeed, might I not now with profit learn something of this style? It was my romantic agonies that had recently seemed both perilous and self-indulgent.

My father's two passions were politics and the pursuit of women. He could play down the importance of the latter by saying that it was trivial in comparison with the former. However in later life he once said to me – Do you think if I had spent less time on women I might have done better in politics? I said – Dad, you might have done much worse! I meant – Surely it had been his willingness to be diverted from politics by life's more sensual pleasures that had made him a relatively harmless fascist leader. He laughed.

And now, in the nineteen fifties, in his middle age, he was entering politics again with a reckless programme aimed at controlling or preventing black immigration. This echoed not only the immorality but the disastrous self-destructiveness of his pre-war anti-semitism. So – would that he might once more be on the prowl with women! And then it might even be possible for me to joke with him about this - in an alternative intimacy to that in which we had once written so portentously about meaning.

And might I myself be diverted from taking romantic shenanigans so ponderously?

After Rosemary and I had settled into Sussex we rented a small flat in London so that we might not be so cut off from social life as we had been in Wales. But we had difficulty in affording this; so when my father, who was by this time domiciled as a tax exile in Ireland, offered to rent the flat from us when we were not using it, and to pay us in cash, this offer was welcome. We assumed that he needed a base from which to run his newly formed Union Movement in London. (But had he not already got a headquarters office?)

Rosemary and I had a slightly disreputable friend at this time whom I shall call Martin. He used Rosemary as a confidante and our house in Sussex as a refuge when he got into sexual imbroglios in London. He had been having an affair with a rich and aristocratic young girl, and he telephoned Rosemary to ask if he could come and stay for a while to get out, as the saying is, of the heat of the kitchen. Also he said he would have some interesting news to tell us. When he arrived, this news was that my father was now in pursuit of the rich and aristocratic young girl, and by the time-honoured method of sending her dozens of red roses. And the girl was responding. So he, Martin, had moved out, but was keeping in touch. So he would be able to give us bulletins about how my father's campaign was progressing.

I suppose it was typical of my state of mind at this time that my feeling about this was just that it would be amusing to have a ringside seat at my father's carry-on; this would provide a change from the lacerations of my own recent style of such involvement. And if the connections between me and Rosemary and Martin and the girl became known, surely my father would think this funny? And I might indeed be able to tease him as he teased me.

There was however an added dimension to this in that my father, now nearly sixty, was involved with a girl not much more than twenty; so that my stepmother Diana, holed up in Ireland, was in the sort of position in which my mother had been some twenty-five years ago when she, Diana, had been in a relationship with my father similar to that in which the young girl was now. So, in this later turn of the wheel, how would everyone react? Could the situation now be seen all round as funny? Before, its results had been catastrophic.

My father occupied the London flat. Then for a while he had to return to Ireland, so I took the chance to spend time in the flat while Rosemary remained with the children in Sussex. I was on my own one evening when the telephone rang and a woman's voice said – Who's that? And when I said who I was, she said she must have got the wrong number. But she did not seem surprised, and she did not ring off; she said she thought I had a nice voice. So we chatted, and agreed that it would be nice if one day we could meet. But nothing more was said. And after we had rung off it struck me that this might well be my father's girlfriend. Did she not know he was in Ireland? Or was she checking up to see that he was? Or might this be the beginning of an elaborate trick or tease?

My memory of just what happened next is uncertain. Did the girl ring again, this time openly? Did I meet her socially – either with Martin or my father? (At some point in this story I have a memory of my father bringing her down to Sussex for Sunday lunch, but I can't place the timing of this, and it seems so unlikely!) Anyway, the next thing I remember in due order was the girl formally ringing me at the flat to ask me out to dinner; and by this time she knew who I was, and even that I knew of her relationship with my father. So either a trick was afoot, or some even more curious convolution.

I went to have dinner with her in her rather grand London flat. (What was Rosemary doing? At art school in Paris? Doing her beautiful paintings of horses by the sea in Languedoc?) At the dinner there was just one other girl and a parlourmaid, or whatever. Then after dinner they disappeared, and there was just me and my father's girl. And she said she had a present to give me, which was in her bedroom.

By this time it seemed clear to me – Of course! My father is wanting to find out whether my Christianity is of the Protestant or the Catholic variety; and so is this a dirty or a witty trick? But in either case, how on earth should I respond? If I turned and ran, I would be Protestant: if I played along, I would be Catholic. But I did not want to be caught by my father's trick! I suppose I wanted to take him on at his own game, and get away with it.

In the girl's bedroom we sat on the edge of her bed and she handed me a beautifully wrapped parcel. When I opened it, it contained a Bible. I said in some amazement 'But you can't give me a Bible!' She looked rather hurt and said 'Why not?' And then – 'Your father said you were religious!' I found I was rather touched by this: Perhaps after all I had got the whole thing wrong and my father was sending me a heartfelt message – even if one of bizarre sophistication! And why should one not treat sexual shenanigans with wit; and even claim that such a style could be Christian? I thanked my father's girlfriend for the Bible, and said that I would be in touch with her very soon to ask her to have dinner with me; but now I had to go.

So – was I being tested not so much about whether in sexual attitudes I was Catholic or Protestant; but rather – did I not agree with my father that most extra-marital sexual situations were basically comic, and should not civilised humans treat them as such? Or would I be shown up as a pompous ass?

But still, how to deal with that one!

When the time came, if I was not to duck the issue, for me to ask the girl out to dinner, I told her that what I would like to do was to take her ice-skating. There was a craze for this at the time which was considered rather vulgar; I said it would be a new and jolly experience for both of us. Accordingly we went to a huge and garish ice-rink somewhere – I like to remember it as Streatham, because I wanted the experience to be working class, but I think it was more likely to have been Queen's Club in Bayswater – and there we hired skates, and held hands, and went round and round. And we slithered and tottered and tried to keep time to the dance music; and we sometimes half fell and had to cling to one another; and so it did seem, yes, that we were having fun, and even in a romantic way which would not otherwise have been available to us. We had supper on the balcony looking down on the gaudy scene; and I told her how glad I was to have met her, and how much I enjoyed being with her, but I must explain that as it happened I only fell in love with working-class girls – and so she would understand, wouldn't she? I don't know if she believed this; or she might have thought I was being clever. Anyway, at the end of the evening she thanked me, and said she had had a lovely time.

Then on the next and last occasion that I bumped into her (she soon went to live and marry in America) she said 'I told your father that you only fell in love with working-class girls.' I said 'Oh Lord, what did he say?' She said ' "I suppose that means he's in love with a working-class girl?" ' And I thought this was clever; and that my father and I had come through this trickiness with some skill and perhaps no loss of affection.

There was one more incident in this saga however of which again I cannot remember the exact timing: but it can be slotted here or there according to what impression a reader wants to take from this story. The occasion was when Rosemary and I were in occupation of the London flat and my father telephoned to say he must see us urgently because he had something important to tell us. So he arrived, together with his girlfriend, and they sat side by side on the sofa demurely; and it seemed to be accepted that none of us were going to say anything about what in fact was going on. My father said that he understood Rosemary and I were friends with someone called Martin; and so he, my father, had come to warn us to have nothing more to do with this Martin, because he had it on good authority that Martin was a blackmailer. (He was not.) My father's girlfriend continued to be silent and enigmatic. Just then there was a buzz from the front door downstairs – Rosemary and I knew that Martin might be coming for a drink that evening, perhaps even to keep us up to date with news about my father – so I went downstairs and there, yes, on the doorstep was Martin. I told him what was going on upstairs, and we both began to fall about laughing. This made so much noise that the occupant of the ground floor flat, who happened to be a fashionable psychoanalyst with whom Martin was acquainted, came out to see what was going on. So Martin said he would tell him the story if he would ask him in and give him a drink; because he, Martin, could not now have a drink with Rosemary and me upstairs. So Martin went in with the analyst (what on earth would have been his interpretation?) and I went back up to Rosemary and my father and his girlfriend. And suddenly it seemed as if the story might not be funny after all; what on earth was my father up to? Might not moralists be right? Or perhaps such a story could properly be seen as funny and intriguing and somewhat squalid all at once. This was what life was like, after all.

But anyway, it seemed to register some further signing off from intimacy with my father. It was no longer easy to tease or joke, just as it had
become impossible to be portentous. And we were none of us seeing
any more of the girlfriend, because she was off on even more bizarre
maneuverings in America.

7

So what on earth should be made of the aforesaid story?

It will be remembered (if the mind has not been turned off by events and attitudes not adding up) that this was occurring not long after sad traumas with my ex-prison-camp girl Mary; after my embarking on an attempt at commitment to Father Raynes. So what was I, a would-be Christian, doing playing around so airily with my father's sexual misdemeanours: should I not be entering a period of rectitude; of sackcloth and ashes? But in the style that I was learning, this did not seem to be called for.

At the end of the war I had written to my old schoolfriend Timmy –

> All that I have learned of men is that they are composed of such a mixture of perfidy and nobility that I cannot hope to unravel, and all I have learned of life is that there is nothing more to be known about it save that which is observable at the end of one's nose.

But then I had come home to the bewildering garden of girls, and had learnt that in peace one had to come to terms with things as neither black-or-white nor incomprehensible, but as paradox.

And so after the confused agonising of my relationship with Mary (I would say to my friend Aelred histrionic stuff like 'I would lose an arm or a leg if I could find a way of being both loyal to my marriage and a saviour to Mary!') it was as if I were being nudged now towards the view that sexual pressures and irregularities did not matter so very much so long as – what – one was attending to the things that did matter? This was my father's view: but then what mattered to him was his baleful politics. Aelred and Father Raynes might have a similar view of the relative unimportance of sexual irregularity, but then what mattered to them were the attitudes of Christ.

Many Christians seem to have become hung up, their sanity addled, about sex. They think that marital fidelity, the condemnation of adultery (indeed of almost any form of sexual activity apart from that offering the chance of procreation) is a bedrock of Christ's teaching. They can dig out of the Bible just enough quotations to give a hard time to anyone who contradicts them. And if one of the latter, overcome by the boredom of the one-upmanship of knocking quotations to and fro, says – All right, call this a bedrock if you like, but in the Bible there are so many other could-be-called bedrocks in apparent variance that it is not by sanctifying one and ignoring others that you will get truth, but rather by taking them all on board in the baggage of your heart and mind – but by this time one will have forgotten the beginning of one's sentence, and others will have interrupted or stopped listening.

In fact (by which is meant 'in the considered aesthetic judgement of the writer') sexual misdemeanours were ones which Jesus himself seemed to find impossible to take with much disapprobation, perhaps because they were related, however ambiguously, to love; and love constituted, in Jesus' view, the nature of God's relationship with humans. The most straightforward instance of Jesus' attitude to sexual irregularity is in the story of the woman caught in adultery. She was brought before Jesus by Pharisees who wanted to catch him out. According to strict Judaic law the woman should be stoned: the Pharisees knew of Jesus' teaching about forgiveness, and they thought he would have to gainsay either the sacred law or his teaching. What in fact he did, it is recounted, was at first to say nothing; then to draw on the ground with a stick as if ruminating or praying or just, yes, bored. He then said to those who were watching 'He that is without sin among you let him cast the first stone'; and went on with his doodling. The crowd melted away. Then he said to the woman 'Where are your accusers? Has no one condemned thee?' And when the woman said 'No, Lord,' he said 'Neither do I condemn thee. Go and sin no more.'

Fanatical commentators on this story are likely to point out that although Jesus did not condemn the sinner, he did condemn adultery by referring to it as a sin and by telling the woman to do it no more. But this ignores the whole atmosphere, the style, of the story, in which the emphasis is on Jesus being so impatient with the irrelevance of what is happening that he has to divert himself by drawing in the dust. (What would his illustration have been – a caricature of one of the woman's accusers? The first lines of a limerick?) Puritans also ignore the paradoxical complexity of Jesus' attitude to sinners: adultery is a sin, all right; but all humans are sinners, and sins related to love are likely to be of less weight in the balance against the vindictive arrogance of people who think they have no sin. At the centre of Jesus' teaching there is the insistence that what matters is that persons should recognise and admit and do something about their own sins; and with regard to others maintain and manifest this attitude. One should try to avoid sin, yes; and there are indeed some sins that humans should not forgive; judgement on these should be left to the Holy Spirit. But there are some sins, yes, that may be seen as fit subjects for a doodle.

It seems to be a limitation of mind that causes confusion among

Christians – the lack of a capacity to distinguish between what is vital and what is not: a failure to see that some things can both matter and not so much matter at the same time. Christ loved the self-admitting sinners with whom he felt at home; he avoided the company of those who would condemn them. He upheld the Old Testament commandments which delineated sin; yet it is explicit in the Gospels that he liked to be with so-called publicans and wine-bibbers; he was scathing about those who were so busy spotting the faults of others that they had no awareness of their own. The message for everyone is – Work for forgiveness – of oneself, of other people. Sin should be avoided; but to be obsessed with condemnation may be the worst sin. Such a paradox breeds uncertainty? Well so it may. Without paradox there is no room for assessment or manoeuvre. There can be no freedom of choice.

To accept this however requires a state of mind adapted to be able to see a situation in two or more ways at once. This is an accomplishment little catered for in the Western rationalist tradition, which insists that something either is or is not; either has to be avoided or does not. Christ seemed to recognise that people, including his disciples, would have difficulty with the different tradition that he was suggesting. But he promised that there would come to their aid the Holy Spirit, who would guide them into seeing things in the way of what might result from them – perhaps going two by two like the animals into Noah's Ark.

There has recently emerged a scientific understanding which accepts the necessity of seeing fundamental things paradoxically in two ways at once – one, the rational determinist cause-and-effect manner of Darwinian evolution; the other a style that recognises a function that some scientists have called self-organisation – this seemingly occurring not only in the formation of atoms, molecules, cells, but perhaps most strikingly in the structure and stuff of the universe – only five per cent of which (it has been claimed) consists of matter conforming to Newtonian laws of physics, the rest behaving in a paradoxical manner and being referred to as 'dark matter' or 'dark energy.' Scientists have found it necessary to assume the existence of these in order to explain how the universe maintains itself in balance as it were rather than either flying apart or contracting to a point – which would be expected according to conventional laws of attraction and repulsion. This state of affairs (not 'either/or' but 'both/and') can be scientifically observed but cannot yet be explained in a traditionally scientific manner. But scientists are apt to turn scornfully on outsiders who they see as trespassing on their preserves, and they cling religiously to that word 'yet.' So perhaps it is polite to shut up, and return to one's doodling.

But this may still be a time and place to utter a cry of anguish against those blinkered fundamentalist Christians who go sailing away on some Titanic into the sunset imagining that they know precisely what God has instructed them to think and to do, precisely what God himself thinks and does; that the Bible is a rule-book that gives God's straightforward (even if often patently contradictory) instructions. And so the Titanic goes floundering on. But thank God, there are life-rafts that can be clung to by those who advocate observation, listening and looking, even in the half-dark; after the fundamentalists have met their icebergs head on.

- 8 -

The person being left out of much of this story is Rosemary, whom I loved and married, and I have always thought this was right so to do. We remained married for twenty-five years, continuing to love but also learning when this seemed sensible to go our own ways. Sensible? Have I not been saying that Christianity is not sensible? Yes. What Christianity says, in the words of the marriage service, is that two people who marry become one flesh, and so in this sense (or nonsense?) they cannot separate, whatever the ways in which life beckons them. And this is what I felt and feel about Rosemary – that in the sometimes vagrant years of our marriage, and indeed when according to the world it was sensibly over, we were like two of those sub-atomic particles which, once they have been together, are in a scientific but nonsensical way always together even if at opposite ends of the universe. (I have used this image before; how pleasant when the imagery of physics can be hijacked to illuminate theology!) Even after Rosemary's and my eventual divorce I continued to visit her and sometimes to stay with her when she became ill; and I was at her bedside with our four children when she died in 1991. And my second wife Verity helped to organise the gathering after her funeral.

Rosemary's and my difficulties had been to do with trying to get the best of both worlds – to be both so-called 'artists' pursuing our visions, and good and faithful family people: both the prodigal looking for experience, that is, and the stay-at-home sibling being loyal. Neither role seemed to us unnatural; it was the combination that was uneasy. We both came from an upper-class background where it was thought natural to want to be adventurous, and yet to have a secure home to return to. However in other ways we wanted to break away from our background – from its dissimulation and hypocrisy. This desire added to complexity. But we neither of us wished to blame the other if we failed.

I had told Rosemary most of what had gone on between me and Mary; she could guess the rest. It had seemed inconceivable to us that for such a situation I might want to break our marriage. Regarding religion, Rosemary once remarked whimsically that things would be easier if Father Raynes were God; but she paid less attention to what he advocated than I did, and perhaps this made things more difficult than they might have been. She seemed to feel that painting was more part of a natural religion: but as I have suggested, it is my job to dwell not on Rosemary's difficulties, but my own.

She came with me and the children to Church; she knelt and said bedside prayers with us in the evenings. And for the rest – why should not painting be part of natural religion? She went to art schools in London or Paris when the situation with the children seemed to permit this: at home she set up, and could retire to, her studio in a spare room. She travelled to France, to set up her easel by the Mediterranean sea. She did not want to waste time being too critical of her prodigal husband.

Perhaps, as Father Raynes had hinted, it may be young children who suffer from their parents' trying to get the best of both worlds. (Our second son in later life remarked of the time after Nanny had gone – Out of the frying pan into the fire! But both he and our eldest son say that they had a happy childhood.) After a series of *au pairs*, we sent our sons away to boarding school at the age of eight or nine: this was what most parents from our background did: but again, had we not wanted to be different? We went as far as to ask for advice from some lay members of Father Raynes's entourage, who recommended a preparatory school where there was said to be a good Christian life centred on the chapel. We sent our second son there for a term or so before it became evident that the clergyman-headmaster was an obsessive beater and was carrying on with the matron, which left little time for teaching. Luckily our unfortunate son did not feel bound by the schoolboy code of not telling tales, so we took him away and found a conventionally fashionable school. Our confidence in church-goers' mundane judgements was dented; but we had not broken away from all the customs of our background.

I became churchwarden of our local Sussex church. I tried, in vain, to instigate some avant-garde innovations such as getting the altar moved more to the centre of the church; to use sheep or goats to keep down the grass in the graveyard. (The objection - 'But what about, you know, the mess?') With more success I took a group of teenage Young Communicants from the parish's working-class housing-estate for a week to Butlin's Holiday Camp at Clacton – together with two of my children and two of my friends with their children. We had a good time. When we asked the official so-called 'red-coats' what they thought of our curious group, they said that they thought that we grown-ups must be on as it were a dirty weekend with the children. We were duly shocked by this. We worked out later that it could have been a joke.

Rosemary and I had our London friends down to stay at weekends. We continued to play our childish and energetic games; also to flirt, but decorously. What else was there socially to do? And our children could be observing and learning for themselves about the oddities of the grown-up world – as my sister and I had had to do.

But what was I learning? To the Church I felt loyalty; but also a rebel. This need not make sense: but it was a paradox I had yet to feel at home with.

In the meantime I was writing my third novel. The first had been published to some small critical acclaim; the second remained unpublished. This third was the one intended to be a semi-coded paean of love to Mary, which would be wafted to her even to the other end of the universe – where we should, of course, still be joined in some neo-scientific affiliation. This novel was in the style of romantic or sentimental tragedy which I hoped might make it a seller. But the literary world was moving into the era of the Angry Young Man.

And then shortly before publication I heard from my publisher that he had had a letter from a lawyer saying that a client was claiming that my book was libellous. His client had got hold of a proof copy, and there was a character in it that was clearly identifiable as herself; and she demanded that the book should be withdrawn. I asked my publisher to put the publication on hold while I inquired into this. It was a serious blow not only to my romantic dreams but my ambitions; I was now in my thirties and had so far published only one book. And I had placed such hopes on my heart-on-a-plate story! But still – might I not now in the course of legal machinations have a chance of seeing my ex-loved-one again, and in an acceptable setting? So might this not after all be a miraculous second-best in whatever was a possible world?

So after a time we did meet, Mary and I, on the neutral ground of the house of a mutual friend; and we were both hollow-eyed and wounded; but under what other conditions could we have met? So had the whole thing – my book, my hopes, her being on the furious look-out for it –

been an intricate, self-organising (as it were) ploy to get us, by a combination of chance (God?) and free-will (so-called), into a position in which we might have a go at sorting things out? What a blessing! (This was a reward for the slog of being a churchwarden? For the success of taking the Young Communicants to Butlins?)

Mary and I faced each other and spoke formally and bleakly like accomplished actors – about possible omissions and alterations by which one day my novel might yet be published. (With the character like herself made unrecognisable – what a thing to want!) But what further might be being worked out? We would still have to wait and see.

After a time my book, *The Rainbearers,* did get published; and I waited. Perhaps we had now to learn, Mary and I, that henceforth this sort of involvement was out of our hands. In the meantime I seemed to be in some sort of limbo with the style of trust that Father Raynes had left in my hands.

I wrote another novel, *Corruption.* This one had a more upbeat end than the one about Mary. However it was still in a tragic-romantic mode, and then I knew I did not want to write any more novels in this style. In the light of what I hoped to experience, and of which I had had some glimmer, it seemed false. Perhaps I needed to look more closely at the way the outside world organised itself and survived; less about my own contortions.

So I went with my friend Hugo Charteris, a fellow novelist, on a four month trip by Landrover around West Africa. He had a contract to do journalism for a London daily: I would write a travel book. We had planned to drive across the Sahara, but the French were testing their atomic bomb there; so we had to leap-frog by boat to Dakar, and then zig-zag east between desert and rainforest. We stayed in huts with tribes who performed their complex rituals to ward off the evil eye and to give life meaning: we attended the stately and equally ambiguous ritual which celebrated the independence of Ghana from the trammels of empire. We saw the vastly intricate beauty and wonder of the natural world: also the hardship and laughter of humans as they just got on with things.

On my return I wrote my travel book called *African Switchback* in which I hoped to portray the roller-coaster nature of experiencing this wild world. But after that, what should I be getting on with?

- 9 -

For some time Father Raynes had been trying to get me involved in some form of Christian publishing. There were plans to make me editor of a new monthly magazine that would challenge, and try to bring back on to hallowed rails, current Church attitudes that could be thought to have become sidetracked. I felt pulled towards the idea; felt ill at ease with it; but what better was there for me to do, if for the moment I had run out of confidence in writing novels? I could play with the children; act the part of a rogue churchwarden; but I had known for some years that I might one day need a more full-time Christian commitment. I enquired about working for Oxfam; about various charities run by Quakers. But they all needed people with professional training. I felt a watershed looming: I was like a man wondering in what way to run from an approaching tsunami.

My London life became more febrile. There was a magical area of Soho at the end of Dean Street where it meets Old Compton Street, where there lurked the Gargoyle Club, the Colony Room, and the pub then called the York Minster. These had become a lure, a home from home, for a raffish and entertaining set of writers, painters, drop-outs; also girls who could drop in here or there on their own – and all the better if they were seen as fallen angels. I had for some time felt that I had a refuge here, or even some never-never-land home – not so much in conflict but in symbiosis with my family home, and a spiritual one perhaps with Father Raynes.

At the Gargoyle Club one night shortly before I was due to be interviewed by a charitable organisation apparently ready to put up money for a Christian magazine, Rosemary and I, together with our friends Sara and Raymond Carr, were performing to the latest hit music of *Rock around the Clock* our interpretation of the ballet *The Dying Swan*. In the middle of this someone tipped off a tabloid Sunday newspaper; and that weekend there appeared a lurid centre-page spread with huge photographs and headings such as 'Rich Layabouts at Play'. The panel of church dignitaries who interviewed me soon after this still offered me (it seems to me to their great credit) an editorial job; though there appeared to be some hold-up about the funding.

I am telling such stories about a somewhat raffish part of my life not so much to give a trendy impression – Oh what a bad boy am I! – as to illustrate what I have been saying about the possible nature and effects, if there is trust, of what can be called sin. I have gone on about how Jesus seemed to like the company of undisguised delinquents; it seemed to be through their open-hearted lack of self-defence that they were able to listen to him and love him, and thus that grace might operate. I was steeling myself for the job of editing a Christian magazine; at the same time I suppose I was keeping an eye out for possible escape-routes. But either step would be a jump into the deep end of a seemingly limitless ocean; so might I not again need to be given a push? When saints had suggested – 'Love God and do as you like' – might this be interpreted as – 'Trust; and then God may catch you with your guard down'?

While waiting for the funding for the magazine I planned to go for a short trip to Berlin to get background for a story I had in mind, which would provide work to fall back on if plans for the magazine fell through. So while still in limbo as it were I went off again to the Gargoyle and there I came across a girl who was less like a fallen angel than a bird of the air or a lily of the field – those whom Jesus recommends us to be like when obediently taking no thought for the morrow. She was on her own, and I asked her to dance, and I told her I was going to Berlin first thing in the morning. She said 'You are lucky!' I said 'Why not come too?' and she said 'I will!' And there she was, on the doorstep of my flat at half past six the next morning, with almost no luggage. And we had a very good time in Berlin.

So what do you think Jesus meant about being like a bird of the air or a lily of the field? You think he was being fey? That was his style?

The point I am trying to make (I say this again and again because people seem disinclined to credit it) is not – Wow! What a good time we had in Berlin! (though this was true) but – Look what followed from it! Christ's suggestion seemed to be that the proper working-out of difficult fate or chance does not seem to favour persons who keep to rules so much as those who trust and are ready to take off and fly. They may crash, be caught by a forest fire. But wounded or singed, there is given a chance to come into operation what Christians call –

Except that Christians don't often talk about the operation of the Holy Spirit; perhaps they don't want to tempt fate.

It was winter and very cold in Berlin. Because my bird-of-the-air had brought no extra clothes, it seemed sensible to spend much of the time in bed. But we did some sightseeing – the Bunker, the Chancelry, the museum in the Eastern Zone. The Wall had not yet been built. Each day my angelic companion telephoned to her regular boyfriend at home to let him know she was all right. I thought – So this, yes, is trust! In the evenings we would go to a café where there were telephone lines between the tables and people kept sending her messages addressing her as Miss Super-Modern.

When we got back to London we told each other what a good time we had had; we did not know when we would see each other again. This was the winter of 1958, and in the spring there was likely to be the first number of my Christian magazine.

Concurrent with this time I was becoming aware of my father's renewed political activity in London. There had been an increase of immigrants from the West Indies and these were settling into the Notting Hill area of North Kensington; here there were disturbances between gangs of white youths and blacks defending themselves. At first these scrimmages had been not particularly unusual; then it was reported that some of the white gangs were being organised by my father's Union Movement. My father's stated policy about immigration was that Britain should invest capital in the West Indies so that there would be jobs which, rationally, West Indians would not want to leave or to which they would want to return. But – I tried to tell him – when have people, or politics, ever been rational? And in the meantime there were photographs in the papers of my half-brothers Alexander and Max in the area as 'observers,' and dressed in the 'teddy boy' style of the time. I had not seen Alexander or Max since they had stayed with Rosemary and me some years ago when my father had asked me to find schools for them in England. I had got them in as boarders at Millfield.

The time now had come when everything was arranged for me to take on the editorship of a small Anglican magazine called *Prism*. This had been started a year ago by two young undergraduates from Cambridge, Christopher Martin and Robin Minney; and it now needed money to survive and to expand. An organisation called The Society of the Faith agreed to put up money if I would put up an equal amount and would become overall editor. I felt that I should not back away from this – partly because I felt I had had such luck with my time in Berlin.

But then my by-now fallen angel with whom I had been so lucky turned up at my flat and said that she was pregnant: she thought the child must be mine, but she must make it clear that she in no way wanted to leave her regular boyfriend. I said I very much hoped that she would not have an abortion, but I would give her sufficient money to be able to do so if she chose; and she could do with it as she liked. She thanked me, and said again what a good time we had had. I was thinking – Well this is frightening; but it is true I have been wanting to find a way in which it would seem proper to give her money. Then she left.

This was Holy Week, 1958. It seemed that I now had two things to do. The first was once more to make my confession; the second, following from this, was to commit myself decisively to the Holy Magazine. There is an Anglican Church called All Saints, Margaret Street, which I knew was often open for people to drop in and make their confession – especially in the climactic week up to Easter when the fate of the world was said to have been decided. So I went there and confessed my goings-on in Berlin and their aftermath; and the priest, whom I did not know, seemed so shocked by my story that I thought he might not give me absolution. (And one is not supposed to say to one's confessor – But only God knows all the ins and outcomes of a story!) But he eventually gave me his blessing; and the next day was Good Friday, when there was to be a big demonstration in Trafalgar Square pressing for unilateral nuclear disarmament, which would be followed by a march to Aldermaston where nuclear bombs were being made. So I thought I would go to this meeting, because although I did not really agree with nuclear disarmament (I thought the existence of the Bomb might prevent the ghastly excesses of so-called conventional war) at least in the Square I would be with people who were concerned with the way in which the fate of the world might once again be being decided.

There was a huge crowd in Trafalgar Square – families with young children in push-chairs or on shoulders. They were listening attentively to speeches from people on the plinth, who were asking – Do you want to live in a world where at the press of a button by a madman you could all be wiped out? No one was answering. I was thinking – But that is not the important question: it should be rather – In what way can an individual have any influence over fate? I found that I was standing next to the regular boyfriend of the girl with whom I had been in Berlin; I knew him well enough to greet him. What I did not know at this time was that the reason why he was so unpossessive about his girlfriend was because he had another girl with a family living just up the road, and he was glad to find occasions to be able to spend time with them. He asked me if I was going to march to Aldermaston, and I said I did not know. I asked him how his girlfriend was, and he said that the day before she had had a miscarriage, and was now resting in bed. I said – A miscarriage? He said – Yes. I asked him to give her my love, and he said he would. The march was forming up, and it was as if the boyfriend and I were finding it impossible to move away from each other. So we set off side by side out of the Square. And we did not talk any more; no one was talking much; people were pushing prams and carrying banners and were wondering, I suppose, about whether they and the world had a chance of being saved. Somewhere around West Kensington the boyfriend flaked off and I found myself continuing with a group of boys and girls carrying a banner saying *Let's Go Back To Bows And Arrows*. The banner was heavy, and I offered to carry one of the poles. I was doing this when, somewhere around Hammersmith, we passed a crowd of young right-wing yobs who were shaking their fists and shouting anti-pacifist slogans. One of them, I realised, was my half-brother Alexander. I smiled at him. He pointed at me and exclaimed 'You!' I called – 'Come and join us!' And he did, for a short distance; and it seemed to me later that this was the sort of gesture by which someone's world might be saved. Then he flaked off. But we had had time to agree that we must see each other again. Shortly after this I too left the march: but it seemed that the point of my joining it had been accomplished.

Now that I was attending to editing of the Holy Magazine I was trying to keep clear of the magic area around the Gargoyle. But I did happen quite soon to bump into my girlfriend from Berlin again. I said to her – 'You've been ill!' and she said 'Yes, I had a miscarriage.' And then – 'It really was a miscarriage! I used the money you gave me to put down the deposit on a flat for me and my boyfriend. I hope you don't mind. Come and see it.' I said 'No I don't mind!' Then – 'In fact I'm very glad!' And I was thinking – You mean, if you and I had not gone to Berlin you and your boyfriend might not now be getting a home; and I might not have made contact with my brother Alexander; and I might not now be putting my heart and soul into my Christian magazine? And oh yes – perhaps one day when Rosemary and I no longer have a London flat, I might be able to come and stay in your flat when your boyfriend is not there.

And indeed in the future this did on occasions happen; to the considerable gratification, it seemed, of all.

So there was surely no need to question any further the details of this apparently miraculous (or not?) story!

10

Anyway here I now was, ensconced in an office like a cupboard at the top of a tall building called Faith House to one side of Westminster Abbey; and there for the next two years I edited my monthly magazine called *Prism*. Squeezed into the small space was also my secretary, Anne Holland, herself a protégé of Father Raynes. We requested and collected articles; I wrote a number myself; we sorted them and sent them off to the printer. The following week we put them into envelopes for subscribers and carried bundles to the post office; also more bundles to selected bookshops who had agreed to have them on display. The circulation was never more than a few thousand: some readers said that they were grateful; some said the contents were blasphemous; many did not seem to know quite what to say. All this seemed to be in keeping with what we were trying to do.

My first leading article was entitled "What's Wrong with the Church," and this set the tone. What I wanted to put over was – What was popularly seen to be Church teaching seemed to have little to do with the teaching of Jesus that we read about in the Bible. The Church went on about laws, morals, injunctions: it saw religion in terms of joining an organisation and sticking to its rules. If there were disputes about these, then the Church had the right to say what God's definitions and decisions were. The Church and the faithful were apt to see religion in terms of a social contract.

The teaching of Jesus, on the other hand, had been concerned with everyone having the task of finding the way of life, of becoming the sort of person through which he or she would discover and carry out what God wished them to be and to do. God had given humans freedom; also the ability to do what was required if this was what they chose. Jesus had promised to make available the Holy Spirit, that is, through whom those who watched and listened to what was going on around them, would find what was to be done. It was from the denial of the Spirit by Church people that there followed their mistaken attitudes and misdeeds for which they should repent.

I wrote –

> The Church today is imagined to have something of the nature of a trades-union of the lily-livered and respectable, and as such to the general public its affairs are of as little interest as would be those of a trades union of boilermakers. The only time that outside interest is aroused is when there are squabbles within the union of a faintly ludicrous nature: disagreements between 'high' and 'low' factions which are observed with the same amusement as those, in the parallel with boilermakers, about who should drill rivets through iron and who through wood.

But if Church people watched and listened, as Jesus had instructed them, then it was by faith, and trust in the efficacy of faith, that things might work out for the best. Mistakes, or so-called 'sins,' so long as they were admitted or at least questioned, could be used. Certain events rather than others, that is, would ensue. Such connections between states of mind and events could not be proved, but there seemed to be such patterning. Coincidences could be felt to have meaning, or not, as one chose.

I wrote –

> I do believe that the spiritual courage and integrity of a hermit, say, in Battersea, can in fact change the heart or alleviate the sufferings of a crippled criminal in Peckham. I believe this because I think it is what the Christian faith is about in distinction from the old Jewish law . . .
>
> And which other way is there of demonstrating one's belief in that wholly vital but at the moment apparently forgotten Person of Western Christendom – the Holy Spirit?

And in what other way could I acknowledge my own experience?

At the end of my two years editing *Prism* I put the articles I had written away and wondered if I would ever look at them again. Then some forty years later when I was digging out my old bits of journalism for possible re-publication, I thought I should look at my *Prism* articles again, though I thought I would find them too naïve. But risking naivety has seldom seemed out of place in Christianity; and several of these *Prism* articles form a section of my book of collected essays.

Then one day when I was editing *Prism* there came bounding into my office a presence, a person, who seemed to fill the small room and overflow it with enormous vitality: this was Mary, my ex-prison-camp loved-one, with whom I had been through so much years ago, and with whom recently I had been in limbo. We had been in contact however at one time by letter since the days when we had been in discussion about my book, and I had been able to help her in practical difficulties about money. And in thanking me she had written –

> Of course there is hope. I am so utterly and profoundly glad that you feel it. I have never wished you other than this sort of hope. I know that I have learned in these six years that there is always at least some hope when a problem is acknowledged; but without this recognition, no real choice and hence despair – much of it, I should imagine, unconscious.

And now – here she was! She had heard I was editing a Christian magazine and had thought this so funny that she had felt she must come and tell me! And oh yes, also tell me that she was now all right, in fact she was very well; she was going to get married, and she hoped to have a child, and this would mean all the world to her; and she did not think she would ever have wanted a child if it had not been for what she and I had been through together.

So – the tiny room at the top of Faith House seeming about to burst with wonder. We murmured that perhaps we should not go much further with one another just at the moment; but we should one day, wouldn't we?

And indeed one day we did. We even managed for a while to have a brief love-affair of a peaceful kind that we might have had years ago if we had not been cast into tragic mould by the wounds of war. But such undramatic matters are not so interesting to talk about; no?

*

My editing *Prism* had meant that I was by now almost completely out of touch with my father. (I had been told by a friend that Diana had remarked 'Nicky's magazine keeps us young!') But then there had been the as-it-were miraculous meeting with Alexander on the route to Aldermaston; and shortly after that I had a letter from Diana saying that Alexander had become ill; my father was refusing to pay to send him to a university on the grounds that he was too stupid. When staying with Rosemary and me Alexander had seemed to be the cleverest teenager I had known: he had for instance explained to me lucidly the differences between Heidegger and Husserl. Now my father was trying to get him apprenticed as a chartered accountant, which was sending him, Alexander, into despair. He had retreated to a bed-sitting room in Pimlico and was seldom getting out of bed. And so Diana asked – Could I help?

What appeared to be my father's jealousy of his clever and handsome son was being exhibited at the same time as his unpleasant and self-destructive political campaign in North Kensington. This was hotting up in preparation for the 1959 general election, in which my father was standing as the Union Movement candidate. In formal statements he was sticking to his would-be rational line about investing money in the West Indies; but to observers and reporters on the spot it seemed obvious that he was courting the anti-black vote. This aberration became interwoven in my mind with his treatment of Alexander, and with the danger Alexander would be in if he stayed under his father's influence. It seemed I should have a confrontation with my father that would be not only about politics, but personal. This would have to be not in the form of rational argument, which my father could swat away like flies, but passionate and outspoken.

So I got hold of Alexander and he came to stay with Rosemary and me in Sussex. He agreed that he should get as far away from my father's entourage as possible – even to South America, where his good Spanish would enable him to find work. I said I would do everything I could to help him with this plan; and I thought that Diana might too.

I went up to North Kensington to hear one of my father's speeches. I did not tell him I was going. I wanted to see and hear the style of what was happening.

How on earth was it that the person who had been so serene and unresentful in prison was now once more acting like an insecure racist with a virulent chip on his shoulder? This was his only chance of getting power? But did he now really want or need this sort of power? It seemed that my father was just choosing to do what he was good at, which was standing on top of a loudspeaker-van and bellowing to an adoring crowd. So this was his addiction?

Anyway, in Notting Hill there he was on top of a van doing his performance; and with a crowd around him some adoring and some hostile but perhaps most just there to savour this nowadays so unusual spectacle. His speech was for a time rational; and it was then difficult to tell if people were listening. He then changed key and went off in scathing style telling stories of black people's supposedly primitive eating habits; of the way in which some black men were said to keep teenage white girls in their attics. The mood of the crowd brightened; this was what they had come for – to boo or to cheer! And I thought – But surely he himself needs to be liberated from this sort of addiction! I had already written to him setting out calmly what I saw as the self-destructive repetitions of his policies. My argument was ignored, or knocked back at me like a Ping-Pong ball. Now I thought that I should go and pick a quarrel; to say that if he did not see the effect of what he was doing, then he was in some sense insane.

I wrote to fix a time to see him. He said he was too busy. I went to his campaign office and said I would wait there until he would see me. I realised I was frightened in a way that I had not experienced since the war: so all right, this was war; but without it, of what worth would be peace? I was told that in his inner office my father was seeing a lawyer; this might even be to do with Alexander. Just before Alexander had been due to set off to South America he had been served with call-up papers for National Service; he was told that these were probably invalid, since he was at the time a resident of the Republic of Ireland. But it seemed that my father had fastened on to this development as a possible means of stopping Alexander getting away; or indeed it could be argued with some rationality that National Service might be good for Alexander. So everything seemed to be on a knife-edge all at once – my need to have an emotional outburst against my father; Alexander's need to get away before lawyers could be brought in to prevent this; my sudden doubt, God knows, about whether it might after all be best for Alexander to do National Service, although this would mean another two years in limbo. Alexander had been due, as it happened, to set off that very morning by train to get at least as far as Paris. I did not know if he had in fact left; or perhaps he had been persuaded to stay to see the lawyer who was apparently with my father now. I felt the outcome was out of my hands – indeed a situation like that of war.

I sat in the ante-room of my father's office where there was a printing press turning out pro-apartheid leaflets about South Africa. When eventually I was let into the inner room, there were my father and Diana and, yes, a lawyer – but no Alexander. My father said quickly that he was expecting Alexander, and did I know where he was? I was trying to remember what time Alexander had said his train would be leaving for Paris. I said that I might know why he was not here, and that was one of the reasons why I had come. Did not he, my father, realise how jealous and destructive he was of Alexander; and this was why Alexander had to get away? My father said –Then you do know where he is? I said – I don't know exactly, but that is not the only reason I have come. I want to tell you that your political campaign in North Kensington is not only immoral but insane; you will be destroying yourself with your racism just as you destroyed yourself with anti-semitism before the war; and if you don't see this that is why you are insane. My father said – So politics is at the back of this! I said – What's at the back of this also is that you're vindictive and a lousy father. I had expected a thunderbolt to descend; but my father just said quietly – I'll never speak to you again.

Diana exclaimed – Oh Kit! (This was her pet name for my father.)

The lawyer looked embarrassed.

My father looked hurt.

I said – Well I suppose I'll always speak to you! Then I left.

The next day I wrote to him saying that I was sorry I had said he was a lousy father, because he had not been this to me. Then I got a letter from Alexander saying that he had caught the train, yes, and was now in Paris. Then I went back to my *Prism* office to write some more stuff, I suppose, about how everything was connected by unspecifiable means to everything else.

Alexander did eventually get away to South America. There he survived, and was adventurous, and made his way up to the United States where he got a place at the University at Columbus, Ohio – an introductory string having been pulled by Diana. The cost of the university was paid by my brother Michael and me. Diana sent him what money she could, which was not much; but she never, as was her way, told my father about any help she gave to Alexander. She tried both to do what she thought was best for her son, and to appear to remain loyal to her husband. But there was debilitating confusion here, because of what was not admitted.

After he had done his course at the University Alexander came back to Europe and family discords and dissimulations continued painstakingly to try to work themselves out. Alexander seemed naturally to wish to stay loyal to his mother; and I seemed to have shot my bolt. My father had failed miserably in his campaign in North Kensington, and after one more election failure he was soon to retire from politics altogether.

Karl Marx remarked that history repeats itself – the first time it is tragedy and the second time it is farce. This seems relevant to my father's politics in the 1930s and 1950s. Marx was a materialist, and indeed it turned out eventually that he had little in his baggage except savagery or farce. I wondered if my father would ever be able to come to look on politics, as he had come to look on sex, as funny; which is what farce is meant to be.

11

This might be a place to pause in my story of the paradoxes of peace – with my convolutions with those who had been girlfriends at some resting place, and my remaining links with my father being at least temporarily severed. And I was settled in a worthy job that combined responsibility with routine. But even with some peace achieved life goes on with its tragedies and farces; it is just that one may reach a state in which it is more easy to stand back from them. However it is impossible to stand all that far back from family life; also in my case there were the ambiguities within my commitment to Christianity. I was not clear whether one's attention should be centred on the commandments of the Old Testament as echoed by the Church, or rather on one's impression of that mysterious being so aptly called a Ghost.

Just as I was beginning to edit *Prism* Father Raynes had died, so my links were now lost with even my substitute father figure. This had not been such a blow as I had imagined; it seemed to have been Father Raynes's task, like Christ's, to bring those who trusted him to a position from which they might go forward on their own. He had given *Prism* its life and his blessing: he might not have found it easy to approve of everything I was now putting into it. On the other hand he might have wanted me to say things he felt he could not say himself.

Towards the end of his life Raynes had been increasingly away from his Community. He had served on committees; had travelled to give courses of instruction at home and abroad. Above all he had liked to stay with his friends in Surrey, with whom he had felt more able to be at ease with himself. In his public pronouncements he continued to advocate straightforward Anglo-Catholic views, but these increasingly seemed at variance with his more open-hearted personal style. Then early in 1958 the Community voted, when the opportunity in due course came round, that he should no longer be their Superior. He then found himself inevitably restricted in his movements and pronouncements. He had never paid much attention to his health; and he soon became ill, and died.

I visited him in hospital just before his death. He seemed to be in some desolation. I did not know if this was in a Christian sense natural – some 'dark night of the soul' to be undergone in emulation of Christ's passion – or if it signified some anomaly in Raynes's nature that had not been resolved and perhaps not understood even by himself. One of his favourite quotations had been that by committing oneself to Christ one would find oneself 'in the glorious liberty of the Sons of God.' He had experienced this at first in harmony with obedience to the Community: then it seemed he had moved towards a more ordinary understanding of freedom.

After nearly two years I was beginning to run out of steam with *Prism*. The main points I wanted to make had been made. It had seemed to me that, according to the story of the New Testament, after Christ's resurrection and ascension this was now the age of the Holy Spirit, in which attention should be paid to its promptings both within oneself and from the outside world; also as a means of understanding the style and import of the story. But (as so often struck me) even by Church people so little was ever said about this. Perhaps the activity of the Spirit was something that could not easily be spoken about; only observed. But it seemed to me that the Church had knowingly usurped the function of the Spirit. I was not clear about what Father Raynes would have said about this.

Then towards the end of my two years with *Prism* the Community, through their new Superior, Father Graham, asked me if I would write a biography of Father Raynes. This was at the suggestion of my friend Robin Denniston, managing director of the Faith Press, a religious publishing house which had offices in the same building as *Prism*'s and on whom I had often relied for advice and information. But on the part of the Community this was an extraordinary act of faith, because it would mean I could learn about Raynes's complex relationship with the Community and the Church and its traditional authority. Also it was a godsend for me because it meant that I could give up *Prism* without feeling I was betraying it. And in fact *Prism* carried on healthily under the admirable auspices first of Robin Denniston, and then of Timothy Beaumont, a young Anglican priest who was soon to become a Liberal member of the House of Lords.

Also, I could now go on a trip to South Africa to do research on the most vital part of Raynes's life, which had been in the 1930s when as a young and newly professed monk he had been sent to the Community's Priory house in Johannesburg, and from there had gone to take charge of the Community's work in the African township of Sophiatown. Here he had built a church, started schools, and initiated legal and welfare services for Africans in the days when the injustices of apartheid were grievous but not yet well known. I would be able to learn how such struggles with the practical world, combined with loyalty to tradition, had perhaps formed the paradoxes of Raynes's character.

Then just before I was due to set off in 1960 – on a slow boat via Ascension Island and St Helena to give me time for rumination – I had a recurrence of the rare and virulent form of malaria that I had picked up in the war and which had never properly been eradicated. I was taken to the Hospital of Tropical Diseases and was set up as a guinea-pig for doctors and students to come and prod and question. In intervals between this and high fever I thought I should take the opportunity to read the Bible straight through. I had for long been amazed how Church people seemed not to encourage this, preferring to listen to it in their services chopped up in bits and pieces. It was in this way, it had seemed to me, that they could take what they liked from it and need not confront what it was saying as a whole.

So off I went on this long journey through myth and history; and yes, I thought I could see how Church people might feel this experience to be a threat to Church authority. This was when it began to seem apparent to me that of course God must have planned for his children to get out of the Garden of Eden: what else should a father do when his grown-up children seem reluctant to leave home? He can't simply throw them out, because this would appear unloving. So you have to think up some trick, eh? Some story about pinching apples? Then the children can blame you secretly, which should help them survive until they find their own feet. They should be grateful after a time – unless they never do find their feet. Oh well.

And the rest of the Old Testament – isn't it the story of God's children always tripping up and blaming God for leaving them with impossible instructions, rather than getting on with finding their own feet? And so by the end of the Old Testament – what darkness! But then God seems to have been feeling a bit responsible after all, because although he had honoured them in guaranteeing them freedom, he had perhaps not given them quite enough information (or guts?) about how to surmount the mechanisms of the natural world; and so instead of finding peace they were always flopping back into war.

So what should God do now – let them blunder on until with their talent for science they invented a doomsday machine? He could then say – I told you so! And then some new species could start again.

But that would be a bit feeble. So should he himself make a demonstration to humans of a proper-style human?

They'd probably kill him.

Oh yes.

But not as Spirit.

No.

So that would be all right then.

*

When I eventually reached South Africa – travelling by air to save time that now seemed to be precious – I stayed in the Community's house in Johannesburg where my old friend Anthony, now Father Aelred, taught in the theological college for Africans of which he was soon to become head. I visited Raynes's old haunts in Sophiatown, now in the process of being demolished having been designated a white area. I was taken to see many of Raynes's old African friends, and I learned what had been his extraordinary influence – not only because of his schools and his churches and his battles with the law, but because he, with two other brethren and in partnership with a group of lay sisters from England, had lived amongst Africans and had exemplified the warmth and care of living in a community. Many of the African leaders who years later were to see the peaceful end of apartheid had grown up at this time in Sophiatown. In later life I once met Nelson Mandela and I asked him if he remembered Father Raynes. After a pause he said 'Ah yes, a good man, a very humorous man!'

While I was in Johannesburg in 1960 there occurred what became known as the Sharpeville massacre in which during a non-violent demonstration against the pass laws and other injustices which restricted movement, some seventy Africans were killed by armed police. This escalated the feeling that the system of apartheid would never change without a massive increase of chaos and bloodshed. In the Community House in Johannesburg where on the evening of the massacre I was having supper with the brethren and black students, there was an atmosphere of helplessness and near-despair. Then when later we were all sharing the washing up the tension was suddenly broken by one of the white brethren, who had previously been an actor, saying in an absurdly camp voice – 'Oh you terrible old black things, why don't you go away and wash!' And after a moment's shock we were all overcome with laughter, falling about and clinging to one another's shoulders.

But still, a wicked political situation has to be rescued by more than politically incorrect jokes, however bold.

Some years after my stay in South Africa – I am telling this story now because it seems to run parallel with what I was learning – my friend Aelred became head of the combined Protestant theological colleges for Africans at Alice, Cape Province. There he became a close friend of Steve Biko, the African leader whose story has become well known. While still a student in the 1970s Biko started his Black Consciousness Movement, the aim of which was to transform the situation in South Africa not by violent nor indeed by conventional political means, but by individual Africans becoming the sort of people, personifying the sort of ideas, that had been set out and exemplified by Christ. Biko had no faith in denominations or dogmas; he wrote that God and God's requirements could be known by paying attention to 'what we know of Christ, and to what was going on around us.' Biko's friendship with

Aelred was such that he came to refer to Aelred as his Father in God. In 1977 Biko was arrested and brutally murdered at the hands of the security police. But his story and influence spread. Aelred, having handed over the headmastership of his college to an African, and while on leave in England and having been banned from returning to South Africa, announced that henceforth he wished to lead a life of prayer and friendship and contemplation, rather than of more extrovert activity. This he came to do, in England. And in South Africa, some dozen years after Biko's death, suddenly and almost inexplicably apartheid crumbled; Nelson Mandela was walking free from prison; and there had been no chaos and little bloodshed.

I tell this story because ever since my *Prism* days I had been saying that there do seem to be largely inexplicable connections between personal attitudes and what happens in the large-scale world. And this is when the story that I am telling here does seem to become less to do with the paradoxes of peace than with my subtitle, the presence of infinity. Of course people are free to call this nonsense; but that is the point.

In the meantime I had undertaken to do what I could to help in a practical way in the battle against apartheid. When in South Africa I had made contact with an organisation which arranged for African students in danger of arrest and imprisonment to be smuggled out of the country by air via Swaziland. So when I was back in England in the 1960s it became my job to meet these refugees at Gatwick or Heathrow, and to look after them until they could be settled into an English university or some Church appointment. In this way I spent a happy day with Desmond Tutu, later Archbishop of Capetown, in the course of ferrying him to a trainee curacy in north London. Then Thabo Mbeki, the future president of South Africa, came and stayed with Rosemary and me in Sussex for ten days while arrangements were finalised for his enrolment as a student in Sussex University. He was nineteen, and had an extraordinary self-assurance and dedication. He and my family got on well together; and my daughter Clare, aged five or six, announced that when she grew up she wanted to marry him.

12

After I had finished my book about Father Raynes, I returned to writing novels. It seemed to me that the kind of understanding I was coming upon – suggesting the existence of effects and patterns beyond the rational reach of words – might be given expression in novels, though of a different kind to the ones I had written. The new style would be one in which connections which could not be expressed didactically might be inferred from the patterns of a story; in these there could be openings as it were through which a reader might recognise something of his own experience, which might otherwise not have been brought into consciousness.

Most novels, being told from what has absurdly been called God's eye point of view, tell stories of humans who are largely helpless; who are seen as reacting to blind chance or to relentless cause-and-effect. This does not represent any view of what Christians should call God, who would surely be hoping for humans to take better advantage of his gifts of freedom and information. But indeed a view of human helplessness does represent a popular misconception of God, by which God can be blamed for what goes wrong and humans can absolve themselves from responsibility. The view that I wished now to suggest in my novels echoed another and more fitting remark of Karl Marx – which was that the task of writers is now not only to describe experience, but to change it.

However if I was going to write novels in a style in which such a view was to be exemplified rather than just stated, how on earth would this be intelligible to anyone except myself, or people with similar experiences? There were novelists – notably existentialists – who aimed for a style in which humans would be aware that they had choices: but without an instinct or examples about how these might be carried out, they – writers and their characters – seemed to be pushed towards despair. Sartre, for instance, when faced in his *Les Chemins de la Liberté* with the task of showing how individual choice might affect large-scale affairs, found he was unable to write his last planned volume.

So what would I be claiming to have an instinct about? The Holy Spirit, about whose activities even the devout seemed to find it improper to talk? The murmurings of physicists about 'dark energy' or 'self-organisation' or 'action-at-a-distance', the evidence for which they might find it necessary to conjecture but which could not be put to the test? And so would not novels presuming to represent such a style be open to the incomprehension and indeed disdain of the conventionally religious and irreligious alike? But so what. Should not this be part of the contention?

The novel that I came to write after I had done my best with *The Life of Raymond Raynes* was called *Meeting Place*. The story concerned a husband and wife who for the time being were separated; they had become dissatisfied with what seemed their isolated family life, and wanted to do good works – the husband in London in an organisation such as *The Samaritans*; the wife to go back to her native America to offer help where there has been a large-scale nuclear accident. Their young son in London is often left unattended; he is attacked by a gang of toughs who have grudge against his father. He comes through; but his father determines to go in search of and to bring back his wife; they can try to look after the world best by looking after their family. He finds his wife in a scene of as-it-were mystical as well as communal desolation: they set off home together. I did not quite know how to do this last scene. I had wanted to convey a sense of resolve through desperation which might be a spur to resurrection.

Some readers appreciated the book, but were likely to overlay it with their own interpretations. My stepmother Diana, for instance, with whom after my trip to South Africa and my openly anti-apartheid stance I had been scarcely on speaking terms, wrote to me to say that she admired the sparse style of my new writing because it conveyed so accurately the social vacuity of contemporary London life.

The novel that I wrote after this was *Accident*, which became for a time the best known of my novels because a screenplay was written from it by Harold Pinter from which a film was made by Joseph Losey. Both of these said how much they admired the book and would aim to keep close to it. But although I was greatly pleased to be associated with Pinter and Losey, and in the film they did indeed use most of the story and the dialogue, the way they saw these turned upside down what to me had been the main point of the book.

The story concerned two men-friends in their early forties, one a writer and the other an Oxford don, who do some philandering with students younger than themselves. This might not have been too serious except that in the course of their shenanigans there is a car crash in which a young man gets killed, and the girl who has been driving is drunk and has no license, and thus may go to prison. The don comes across the overturned car which had been on its way to his house, and he realises that no one but he need know that the girl was in the car;

it could be thought that the young man had been driving. He carries the girl up to his house and puts her to bed. He rings up his friend the writer who has been having an affair with the girl; he tells him what has happened, and asks him to come round to try to decide what to do. The climax – indeed the point of the book – is the long and painstaking conversation that the don and the writer have in the middle of the night aimed at coming to a view of what properly and morally should be done; their talk is in contrast to the play-acting (indeed Pinteresque) style of their conversation while philandering. They decide, after much soul-searching (they will thus also be protecting themselves) to say nothing about the girl to the police when they arrive, and indeed at the inquest, unless they are asked a direct question; in which case they will give a truthful answer. This seems to them proper. There is thus a chance that the girl's life may not be ruined – nor their own lives and that of their families harmed. And the young man is anyway dead. But this further outcome will be largely, as it were, in the lap of the Gods.

In the script and in the film this whole conversation was omitted. The involvement of the girl is not discovered, and she returns home to her native Austria. But this happens as it were blindly, without the two friends considering responsibility or the possibility of choice. And in the meantime the don has taken advantage of the girl while she is lying semi-conscious on the bed, and virtually rapes her. This was most vitally not in the book. So the two men, with guilt unconsidered and unresolved and indeed added to, are left – in Pinter's words in a letter to me – 'carrying the can' and 'facing a blank wall.'

Pinter explained that he had tried to put into the script the long conversation between the two men, but he had found this impossible; it was not his style. And about the don going to bed with the girl – well, this had just seemed to him humanly inevitable.

However it was a clever script and a clever film. And indeed, as Pinter said, writers do have different ways of seeing the world.

After this I wrote a novel called *Impossible Object* – an impossible object being something that can be drawn in two dimensions but cannot exist in three – that is, it can be a work of art but not a reality apart from this: or can't it? The 'impossible object' in the book is a love affair between a married man and a married woman in which the man is saying – Look, let's make the best of what we've got and not try to eliminate all difficulties by trying to make it perfect. And the woman is saying – No, why should not love be all-of-a-piece and perfect? So they have a go at this (or do they?) and everything goes wrong (or does it?). The man writes a story of the affair which ends with an incident in which the young baby born to the couple drowns in a boating accident. In the book there is a postscript in which the man says to the woman – Well you used to like unhappy endings, so I have given you one. In the filmscript I wrote from the book (the script was written for Losey, but the film was eventually made by John Frankenheimer) the man comes across the girl again after several years at an outdoor café in Rome and she says to him (following on from the conversation in the book) – What would be a happy end? And he says – This. He sits down beside her; and they watch a child playing at a fountain in the square. This appears to be in 'real life' the child that in the story was said to be drowned.

This book got appreciative if slightly baffled reviews. It was reviewed by a member of the Community of Resurrection who said that it ended in death and despair. When challenged by Aelred, he admitted that he had not read the postscript.

The film was made with a good cast. But it missed the being-able-to-see-things-in-two-ways point of the book, and it too played down the potentially on-going end. When I remonstrated with Frankenheimer about this he said – 'Let's face it, Nicholas, it's a great love story! No one's going to look beyond the death of the child.'

*

So there we were – a would-be serious work of art cannot be believed to have a happy end; such is reserved for sentimental fiction. (Jane Austen? Or does one sense that her happily marrying couples will inexorably dissolve into the banal style of their parents?)

But what was happening in the great big world at this time?

These were the years of the Vietnam War; and of demonstrations against it in which student protestors got killed. The excuse for the war was the threat of what was called the domino effect – the idea that if Vietnam was allowed to fall into communist hands, then it stood to reason that neighbouring countries would follow suit – flopping like a line of vertical dominos until, by an admittedly bizarre route, a last massive tile would crash down on America. I remember arguing at the time – perhaps to annoy people who thought arguments for the prevention of war as well as for the making of it should be a matter for rationality – that I did not think the Vietnam War was altogether a bad thing, because it seemed that humans, with their insane predilection for war, had to have conflict going on somewhere; and if there was going to be war between a communist state and America, then at least Vietnam was comparatively out of the way. It seemed people thought I was joking, and perhaps I was. I had a vision, yes, of history endlessly repeating itself as tragedy or farce: but if one saw it literally as farce, might it not after a time lose its potency?

Might not God, that is, in near-despair at humans' relentless pursuit of disaster, think that their best hope might be if he helped them see this in terms of *commedia dell'arte*? In this there are displays of savagery and insanity; but these are seen archetypally as if through the wrong end of a telescope; and thus they have a chance of appearing, if not un-equivocally funny, perhaps as a form of ironic if absurd admonition.

Or might not God's incomprehensibility, in other but still hardly ac-ceptable words, include the provision that we might be able to see some serious things also as jokes?

In the meantime, and contemporaneously with *Accident*, I wrote a non-fiction work, *Experience and Religion*, which signified the loosen-ing of my ties to conventional 'Church' Christianity, and tried to put as clearly as I could my continuing commitment to what seemed to me to be its essence. This memoir that I am writing now tells of the biographi-cal background to this. *Experience and Religion* was my first attempt to express what I have continued to try to elaborate – the precedence of paradox and learning over certainty and dogma, as demonstrated in the life and teaching of Jesus. One sympathetic review was headed simply – *Saying the Unsayable*.

13

The idea that many of the maneuverings of life could be best seen in the light of *commedia dell'arte* had seemed recently relevant to my dealings with my father; and not only in his sexual shenanigans but even – however violently I had shown my disapproval of them – in his political activities. There was a sense in which even before the war he had come to be seen as less of a serious politician than a one-man band; he had taken little trouble to work at the daily grind of politics – the patience in committees, the currying of favour, the wheeler-dealing for votes – his style was to set out proposals in lucid or rousing oratory, and then just to dump his audience with – Take it or leave it. Once he had abandoned the main parties he never got near getting back into Parliament; nor did any of his followers ever get a place in local government. His role model at least in later life (he himself hinted this) seemed to be Mephistoph-eles in Goethe's *Faust* – whose function was not so much to wield or organise power as to act as a potent gadfly to stir a sluggish humanity to confront their situation themselves. Hence my father's extraordinary cheerfulness even when his plans came crashing down and he was in prison. And it was because of this I was able to contemplate a possible *rapprochement* with him once he gave up, as he had had to do before, his ludicrously self-destructive public activities.

In my personal life I had become aware of the paradoxes of Christianity; but now, well into my forties, I began to wonder if I might ever enjoy again what I could look back on as the blissful chance-effects of romantic agony. I had not yet got much of a feel of the potency of *commedia dell'arte.*

Then in the mid-1960s, just after I had finished *Accident* and *Experience and Religion,* there was a fancy dress party in Sussex to which I went dressed as a clown. I wore a grey top hat, striped rugby jersey, and my father-in-law's white polo breeches. And there I met a girl dressed as Columbine in a tutu. I had seen her once before in the York Minster pub in the magical corner of Soho; and I had thought her then one of the most beautiful people I had ever seen. This was in a gut-wrenching, archetypal way; but as if she herself were hardly aware of it. I had said to whomever I was with – perhaps my Berlin girl? – Good heavens, who's that? And got the reply – She's so-and-so's wife, you've got no chance with her, he never lets her out of his sight. I watched her cross the road and she had a way of walking that seemed to drag me after her hooked like a fish.

The point of *commedia* is that it portrays stock characters in a formalised style that demonstrates the helplessness and even ridiculousness of human behaviour – the contradictions between its swaggering pretensions and the humiliating reality. Yet the characters can improvise; and thus have the chance of free-will. Lovers are portrayed as Harlequin and Columbine – the former clumsy but bold; the latter naïve but scheming. Such characterisation represents humans typecast by conditioning. And how much do humans have freedom?

At the fancy-dress party I asked the girl dressed as Columbine to dance. It was as if she might never have danced before. During a Viennese Waltz it seemed easiest to whirl her round by lifting her off her feet. After this we went for a walk in the garden. I did my usual patter – It would be nice if we could have lunch in London! She said – Why bother about lunch? I did not think I could have heard this right. I said – Well at least a drink. She looked as if she might not have understood me. But I was, yes, a fish in the bottom of a boat and flapping.

Back at home I did not in fact get in touch with her at once; there were too many alarm bells ringing. I should surely be saying to myself - Look what happened last time! Then there arrived through the post a copy of a book that the girl and I had talked about in the garden – *Jacques le Fataliste* by Diderot (I had hardly heard of it). And only half concealed on the first page of text was a hand-written London telephone number. I thought – Good heavens! This sort of thing had not happened to me before. But there seemed something unstoppable about it. So I rang the number, and we arranged to meet in London – for what could be called a pre-lunch drink. And then when we were in the bar of a hotel in Piccadilly I said – Look , there are just one or two things I must tell you –

– Yes?

– The last time something like this happened –

– Something like this happened?

– It was near disaster –

But I did not feel I could go on with this.

So we skipped lunch, and booked into a hotel room.

What in fact was happening, I learned slightly later, was that some time before the fancy-dress party the husband of this girl (I shall call her Natalie, after a character in the novel *Natalie Natalia* I wrote later) – the husband of Natalie had left her and had gone off with another woman. Then after a week or two he had wanted to come back. So she had made a bargain with him – He could come back on condition that he would allow her, without fuss, to have one love-affair herself. Agreement about this had been reached on their drive down to the party in Sussex. Thus it was that I had been hooked and landed as the lucky victim.

In the hotel in London, after we had somewhat perfunctorily (surely understandably) made love, she cried. I said – Why are you crying? She said – That was not so very different. I wondered if I should feel insulted. But I was so grateful! And then she told me of her bargain with her husband.

So what should I now do, as a clown?

What did she mean – That was not so very different?

She had never been much interested in sex? That was why her husband had left her?

But she was so beautiful! (She also, I soon learned, was highly intellectual, wrote poetry, played the piano, and painted.)

So come on, Harlequin: pull up your socks.

But what might socks mean in these circumstances?

A bit of expertise beyond that of *commedia dell'arte*?

I said – Let's at least meet just one more time.

She might have said – Why? But she agreed.

I thought – So now let me run through my memories, limited experience, books (dirty books?). How do people in such a context pull their socks up?

Anyway the next time – but less as a result, I am sure, of memories, experience, as of my growing love not just of her beauty but of her boldness, her readiness to take risks –

After the next time she said – What are you going to do if I fall in love?

And I said – You mean you are not in love? How disgraceful!

This was more the style of *commedia*?

We met a few more times; and then we decided not to see each other again. Indeed this was all too like what had happened before with Mary.

In *commedia* the same situations are repeated over and over. But there is always the chance of fate providing an improvisation.

Some time later I heard through a mutual friend that Natalie's husband had left her again – this time for good, he was saying, because his bargain with her had been for her to have a one-night-stand, not to fall in love. And so he had gone off with yet another woman, and Natalie was sitting at home with her two children and was too proud or honourable to get in touch with me. But she might also be, our mutual friend suggested – suicidal?

So it took not much improvisation from me to get to see her again.

I then rented a flat where I could work and be near her in London. I began to write *Impossible Object.* I thought – An art-work can possibly save one from lunacy! So when Natalie was not visiting me in the flat, I lay for hours in the bath and the impossible but luminous stories of *Impossible Object* seemed to distil themselves in drops on the ceiling and fall on my head. Life was impossible, yes. But one got on with it.

Then Natalie's husband returned and begged her again to have him back ('Think of the children!'). So once more we stopped seeing each other. I could get on with my book: but I felt increasingly demented. ('Hooked and flapping' is a good image, yes.) I would go for long walks – up to Kensington Gardens, along to Brompton Cemetery, where at one end among the elaborate tombs there would be on certain days what sounded like ghostly laughter or angels cheering. After a time I worked out – the Chelsea Football Ground.

And then her husband said he was going off with someone else again.

Rosemary by this time was naturally getting fed up; she had too much of her own serious motivation to be at home in this sort of *commedia*. And with the children growing up it was now easier for her travel to her painting-grounds in the South of France, and to spend time there free of the antics of others.

But then to Natalie and her husband the repetitions were becoming wearisome. There came a time when he said to her – Why does it always have to be me who leaves home? So she and her children came to take refuge in my flat. But I wished neither to seem to be breaking irretrievably with Rosemary nor in these circumstances to be inflicting myself on her; so I went to a bed-sitting room in Bloomsbury to finish *Impossible Object*, where I hoped none of the other *commedia* participants would find me. Here there was another nearby cemetery to walk around; and a gas stove in my room by which I could imagine placing my head if eventually necessary. I was pleased with the way *Impossible Object* had turned out; but in the real world I seemed to have landed myself without a home.

Then out of the blue a letter reached me from an old girlfriend with whom I had once dallied very briefly in my Soho days, who said she had quarrelled with her current boyfriend and was on her own in Paris, and why didn't I come and visit her? So I flew to Paris and we went on a walking tour in the Vosges mountains in thick snow; and we got as far as Colmar where there is Grunewald's marvellous triptych of a tortured crucifixion which I had always wanted to see. And at the end of this trip we said to each other what a good time we had had, as indeed had been said by me and my Berlin girlfriend before. And this time there did not seem to follow anything urgently requiring confession. For by the time my companion was back in Paris, and I was on my way back to London, both Rosemary and Natalie who was still in my flat were anxious about what had become of me; so I became on quite good terms with each of them again.

Talk about *commedia*. Talk about impossible coincidences and chances.

You can risk a few jumps in life as if it were a work of art –
And trust that one day the water will not have been drained from the
deep end of the pool.

*

Somewhere about this time Rosemary's mother died, and amongst
other things left her some farms she had bought in the Isle of Man for
the purpose of avoiding inheritance tax. When Rosemary went to visit
these farms she fell in love with the place, and wanted to keep a farm
and live there – in order to paint the wild landscape, and doubtless to
get away from the increasingly lunatic routines going on in London
and elsewhere. So she and I set about packing up our once much-loved
Sussex family home so that Rosemary could move to the Isle of Man,
where we all might stay in the holidays if things worked out this way;
and I would look for a house in London which could also accommodate
Rosemary and any or all of our children when this suited them; and
possibly Natalie and her children if and when they became otherwise
homeless.

I could afford to look for this sort of house now, because almost contemporaneously with the death of Rosemary's mother, the last of my
mother's aunts had died in America, and in theory there could now be
distributed the capital from the trust that had been set up by my mother's millionaire grandfather in Chicago, and from which as one of the
beneficiaries I had for so long and so gratefully been getting income.
However there had been some anomaly in my great-grandfather's will,
and different branches of his by now extended family were threatening
legal action against one another and if necessary against the trustees, if
their particular interpretation concerning the distribution of the capital was not met. The trustees some years before had warned the po-

tential beneficiaries (some twenty-four in both England and America) that if they did not come to some agreement amongst themselves it was likely, indeed almost certain, that all the considerable capital of the trust (some twenty million dollars) would be swallowed up by the endlessly protracted manoeuvres of lawyers – in the manner of the *Jarndyce v Jarndyce* case in Dickens's *Bleak House*. My sister and brother and I, as great-grandchildren, were minor players in this crisis (our share was some thirty-sixth); but I looked with fierce alarm at the likelihood of soon having prospects of neither capital nor income.

The trustees called for a meeting in Chicago of all the beneficiaries to try to reach agreement; but it seemed that most of these were so adamant that they were proposing just to send to the meeting their lawyers with clear instructions against compromise. So in the manic state of mind I was in as a result of my obsessed ups and downs with Natalie – that of clown, juggler, someone who might well think he could get away with jumping and swimming across the pool beneath Niagara – I announced that I would go to Chicago and represent the branch of the family consisting of my surviving aunt and my siblings – and I did not want anyone to come with me because this might cramp my inflated style. Oh well all right, yes, a lawyer – but I thought on my own I might have a chance of doing the trick. My aunt and my siblings had little reason to believe me, but were perhaps grateful not to be involved themselves in this fraught occasion. So I set off for Chicago followed by just our wise family lawyer, who agreed to let me do most of whatever talking came our way. And when I got to the meeting I found that I was, yes, the only member of the family that was there; the other participants were lawyers. And so I might be in a somewhat magical position, might I not, when I got up to do my talking?

I do not think I have yet mentioned that I still had at this time a bad stammer. This had played a considerable part in my *Time at War*: officers are not expected to stammer, and in fact at moments of crisis I did not. But at humdrum lectures my sergeant had sometimes to bang on the table with his stick to call to order my platoon who were having difficulty not to roll about with embarrassment and laughter. And now here I was to address a gathering of Chicago lawyers.

As I had learned from a worthy psychoanalyst, a stammer can be a mechanism to disarm the potential hostility of others; also perhaps to disguise one's potential hostility to them. Confronting the Chicago lawyers I was in any case an absurdity – a toff from England with no experience of law or local conditions. What I had to say was – 'Look here, this is not really a matter of one branch of the family getting a bit more money than another; it's a matter of either the family getting some money, or you lawyers getting the lot. As I understand it, there have been some negotiations for compromise, and the two sides are only a comparatively small figure apart. So why can't we just split this difference; and surely you lawyers will still be in for a good whack.'

This was good sense, but it had not yet been welcome. What was required for it to be effective was some sort of performance. But when a stammerer is in desperate flood as it were it is nothing if not a performance: he is indeed in the pool at the bottom of Niagara; he flounders, he chokes, he can't breathe, he seems to be making it plain that he is drowning. So after a time, to be sure, his audience may wish to do almost anything to shut him up – even, as a last resort, to help him out. When I sat down there was a silence; then a man who seemed to be the *doyen* of the lawyers said – Well, we can recommend to our clients that they should compromise; but as you know, there is one important family beneficiary who has sworn never to give in. I said – All right, I'll guarantee to sort him out. The gathering now looked sceptical as well as embarrassed. But they gave me a couple of days to try to bring this one person round.

I have told the second part of this story in my *Efforts at Truth*: and too much repetition of *commedia* becomes wearisome. I did manage to get the recalcitrant negotiator – a dedicated gambler – to agree to compromise; first by accompanying him to a shady nightclub to which he had taken me to get me drunk, and there his finding that as my host he had to rescue me from being beaten up. Then later by my storming out of his house in a Washington suburb in the middle of the night exclaiming that I could not bear to spend another minute under the roof of a businessman so hopeless at recognising favourable odds. He pursued me in his huge car and said – What was that compromise figure you mentioned: not bad, eh? *Commedia* should not become a model for every role; but I like to be reminded that there can be some weird empowerment (not grace; no?) if one takes a plunge, goes out on a limb, even in a most unlikely environment. In war, in love, all right: but with Chicago lawyers? Anyway, it had worked. Perhaps those who risk exposing themselves to ridicule may inherit at least their own rightful bit of the earth.

14

Back in England, when my share of the capital finally did come through, the London property market was at its post-war lowest, so I was able to buy an elegant house in Hampstead's Church Row, which even had two studio-cottages at the bottom of the garden – so there could be room for whatever bizarre family maneuverings continued both with my old family and now Natalie's. And thus when Natalie's husband became adamant once more that he wanted a divorce, and Rosemary was settled into the Isle of Man, Natalie and her children moved into my new house in Hampstead, and things in this way for a time seemed to have spaced themselves out.

Shortly before this – just before, in fact, my trip to Chicago – my aunt Irene Ravensdale had died, and thus I inherited the barony that my grandfather Curzon had created in 1910 which could pass down for just one generation through the female line. His eldest daughter Irene had died childless, and I was the eldest son of her next oldest sister, my mother, who had died in 1933. The business of becoming Lord Ravensdale seemed to me in tune with *commedia*; though it was taken with much seriousness by my lawyer and by someone called the Garter King of Arms. I was aware that I had six months in which to renounce the title if I wished (I foresaw correctly that it would do me no good as a writer), but I thought it would be more pompous to renounce it than to keep it, and of course I would retain my Nicholas Mosley name as a writer. I rather liked the idea of having two identities to move between; also I enjoyed designing for myself a coat of arms, which I did in consultation with the person whom it was customary to address as just 'Garter.' The arms incorporated an eagle (the Mosley crest) a popinjay (Curzon) and a raven (myself). Then I was introduced into the House of Lords as a Liberal peer, sponsored by my godmother Violet Bolnham Carter and my old friend Timothy Beaumont who had taken over the running of *Prism*. But I found it impossible to settle into the style or work of the House of Lords; there were a lot of good and serious people doing good and serious work on matters of detail; but it is the role of a politician to argue on one side of a question or another, and not to ruminate, as writers should, on both or every side. But I was glad to have the right of access to the gallery of the House of Commons, which I used to get copy for my novel *Natalie Natalia*.

So with life in Hampstead settling down, my older children came and went during their holidays from school; my daughter Clare made friends with Natalie's son who was of her own age; we were looked after by my housekeeper June who had been Rosemary's and my daily help in Sussex, and was now installed in the basement at Church Row with her husband coming and going from Sussex. In the drawing room there were the beautiful paintings and pieces of furniture that Rosemary had inherited from her mother and grandmother; they could not be taken to the Isle of Man without paying the inheritance tax from which they had been exempted. So things made some dramatic sense, even if on a tightrope.

But then – it seemed inevitably – Natalie's husband once more wanted her and the children back; and there were the usual threats and pleadings and thus crises of conscience. And at these times I was liable to become distraught and would exclaim – All right for God's sake go! – and so Natalie would. And then I would go striding about Hampstead Heath at night where there was an old man like King Lear shaking his fist at the sky and shouting – Why? Why? And I would want to shout back – Why not? But by that time of course I was missing Natalie insanely – how was it that a sexual obsession could be so volatile! And then after a time Natalie's husband would or would not have gone off again – one lost attention to detail – and so Natalie did come back. And it seemed this might go on for ever. But indeed – why not? For it is the style of *commedia* to act out ludicrously and endlessly what seems to be the chaotic nature of human emotions and contradictions; so that in spite of hurt and uproar, there is some sense of – well, this is what life is like!

And there were compensations. During Natalie's absences I could go up and spend part of the children's holidays in the beautiful wildness of the Isle of Man; there I did landscape gardening; I wrote part of *Natalie Natalia* in a tumble-down cottage on the edge of Rosemary's land. And with Natalie gone, Rosemary could stay in Church Row when she came to London. My eldest son moved with some friends into one of the cottages at the bottom of the garden, and there they held a riotous party one night; and some of the neighbours complained. So I made friends with the neighbours and asked them to dinner; but they could never quite be sure who would seem to be their hostess – Natalie or Rosemary, or indeed sometimes June.

And nowadays when Natalie came or went she had to be accompanied by her grand piano, because she was taking lessons from a concert pianist. So the piano was transported to and fro across London on a mobile crane and hoisted up to or down from the window of my first-floor drawing-room. The second or third time this happened the operator of the crane, a phlegmatic man, remarked 'This piano goes up and down like a yo-yo.' I thought this very witty. Such were the compensations of *commedia*.

Quite often jolly for the actors perhaps. But what of the children?

I had had the belief, or hope, that so long as there was no intended deceit or self-deceit in marital uproar, children might not suffer too much harm; might even usefully learn from their parents' convolutions. This may or may not have truth in it. It was my gloss on Jesus' intimations that less harm was done by people who recognise themselves as sinners, than by people who insist that they are not. With regard to my own children in later life and indeed Natalie's children, their rackety upbringing does seem to have encouraged them, in their various styles, to become admirable parents.

The point of history repeating itself the second time as farce is that although much of the stage-business is the same as that of tragedy – people make fools of themselves; get betrayed, trapped – yet because it is all so out-in-the-open, so patently daft, an audience – the participants themselves in their pantomime roles as audience – can feel it proper to laugh. I have come to think that some of Shakespeare's tragedies that most ostensibly portray evil – *Othello*, *Macbeth* – would be better done as farce. As tragedies they seem to give authority to creepy lunacy. But can suffering be done as farce? There is a gloss on Christian theology which claims that after Christ's resurrection there can properly be no more tragedy.

When Natalie had returned and seemed to have settled in again – the piano having once more risen like a yo-yo – she and I would go on art-viewing tours through Europe. We drove down through Italy to Naples; we went by train to Eastern Europe. On the latter trip – on our way back from Prague, Dresden – I took her to lunch with my father and Diana in their home at Orsay, outside Paris. Natalie, who was Jewish, had wondered how I would take her wish to meet my father: I had said – Oh they won't mind us not being married! In the event the lunch went well, with Natalie and my father capping each other with quotations from Goethe.

Shortly after this however I received a letter from a lawyer saying that Natalie's husband was claiming damages from me on the grounds of alienation of his wife's affections. Well, however depressing this might be, as soon as it got into the hands of lawyers it surely would become farce. Natalie and I sat in an office and were taken through details of our journeys through Europe; the ups and downs of the piano. – You say you travelled together to Orvieto, to Volterra? – Oh yes, to see the Signorellis, the Etruscan tombs. – But did intercourse occur? – Oh yes, yes, intercourse occurred! – But you say that this was when your husband had already gone off with –

– Wasn't it in the Villa Giulia in Rome that there was that tomb?

– Oh yes, her husband had gone off with –

– I mean it wasn't Volterra –

– Who? –

– What? –

– I mean the tomb.

So after a time the lawyer would say –

– I really don't think there's a case to answer here.

But the hounds of heaven or hell were breathing ever more openly and dramatically down our necks. The lawsuit was dropped; but the flames of our conscience were fanned.

The day came when the piano was once more being lowered out of the window on its string and I was declaiming – This is it! The end! I can't go on! And I watched the transporter like a hearse go trundling on its way.

The next day, as it happened, I was due to go to a location near Bath to do research for a television script about a pop concert (of all things!) for which I had been commissioned. I had been flattered by this request; and I was now banking on this work to carry me through the despair that at any moment would surely engulf me as a result of Natalie for the umpteenth time having departed, and each time it seeming more likely that she would not be coming back. But coincidentally with the news about the pop concert I had heard that my old Nanny had died – she who had done so much to save the lives of me and my sister and my brother before and after my mother's death, and whom I loved – and her funeral in Welshpool was on the same day as the concert near Bath. So was I not in honour bound to go to the funeral? But what if I missed this chance that might not only set me off on a new line of work but might divert me from the torments of ever more painful farce? I chose to go to the concert (my excuse – Jesus' succinct advice: Let the dead bury their dead). I was on the way to Bath with my second son Ivo and his current girlfriend in the back of the car, when the feeling began to overwhelm me – But of course this is wrong! I should have gone to the funeral! This is a sin for which I will not be forgiven! And then also – Of course I want Natalie back! Guilt and pain and the feeling of having got myself trapped began to build up to a level which seemed far beyond the limits of farce. I was driving slower and slower; it seemed too late to turn round; and anyway the traffic on the narrow road to the concert was so thick that this would have been impossible. I was saying to myself again – I can't go on! I want to give up. But what did it mean to give up? How can fate, farce, be taken out of one's hands? The lines of traffic in both directions had slowed almost to a halt. Then there was a car pulling out from the line coming from the opposite direction; there was no room for the car to get through in the middle of the road. I thought – What is this, a juggernaut? The car was coming straight at me accelerating fast. I must have tried to pull off the road into the ditch because when the car hit me it crashed into my driver's side door. My arm and leg and several of the ribs on my right side were broken: however I acted as a buffer as a consequence of which my son and his girlfriend were comparatively unharmed. But I only learned of their merciful deliverance and of my injuries later, because I became immediately unconscious.

15

Any hope of being able to experience suffering as farce is greatly helped by massive doses of morphine.

When I regained consciousness there was a small crowd around me of ambulance men and breakdown men with their heads down by the foot-pedals. I had been woken by pain, and I yelled. Someone said 'We're trying to get your leg out!' I said 'Well try to get it out along with the rest of me!' I thought this witty. I imagined I might continue – I was expecting something like this, you see; I had been behaving badly; making mistakes; a great juggernaut must have run over me. What is a juggernaut, do you know? Something beneath the wheels of which devotees of a dark god throw themselves? But what does the dark god offer besides pain and retribution: forgiveness? And so on. But then pain overcame the morphine and I passed out again.

I had just managed, I think, to establish that my son and his girl-friend had incurred only minor wounds; so that was all right. When I came round again I was in what looked like the annex to an operating theatre; and I could think – But seriously, can I not make out that this is for the best in the best of all possible worlds? I have been wishing to give up; that everything should be taken out of my hands. And now I suppose they are; I am at least heavily sedated.

The next time I woke I was in a hospital ward and there was a family of strangers round my bed; they were inquiring solicitously after me. I thought – That is uncommonly kind! Or have I floated away under the anaesthetic and have come back into another body? The people round me were saying – We do hope you are all right! I learned later that they were the family of the man who had run into me and who was in the same ward, and they were worried that if I died he might be charged not just with dangerous driving but with manslaughter.

The ward was the long Nissan Hut of an old army hospital. I was at one end amongst elderly men who mostly had tripped in their bathrooms or on their garden paths, and had broken their femurs. They were strung up, as I was, on what is called 'traction' – a contraption of struts and pulleys from which broken bones are suspended until the time comes for them to be mended. At the other end of the ward were young men with broken ankles and tibias, often from motor-cycle accidents; they could commandeer wheelchairs and whizz up and own the central aisle of the ward as if on a speedway track. This caused consternation amongst the old men who feared that the chairs would crash into their traction, which enabled them to be in not too much pain so long as they could remain still, but any movement caused the jagged bones to rub on nerves and was agony.

And anyway, at least once a day the terrible moment came when one had to be washed ('I'm perfectly clean!') and one watched a posse of determined nurses moving from bed to bed ever closer to one's own. ('You don't want bed sores, do you?') There was an old man in the bed opposite me who, when two pretty nurses began to lift him, would cry out 'Oh you buggers! You buggers!' and the man in the next bed, who was said to be a clergyman, would say 'That is one thing they are not!' But it did seem that if one yelled this alleviated the pain. Or should one be like St Lawrence on his grid-iron, who was supposed to have blessed his torturers?

A more urgent problem occurred when at a certain time each evening the man next to me began to try to get out of bed. He did this by pulling on the wires of his traction; then when he realised this was like trying to lift himself by his own bootlaces, he leaned over to get better leverage with mine. I then did feel justified in shouting for help. The nurse who came explained – 'It's just that at this time he used to go every evening for his Guinness.'

The nurse who did most to cheer us up was a wonderfully camp man who would wake us in the morning by posing in the doorway with a hand on his hip and saying in an exaggerated Mae West voice – 'Hullo boys!' And we would all cheer and go – Woo woo! I was reminded of the monk in Johannesburg who had seemed to lift some of the curse hanging over his brethren and his African students by exclaiming – You terrible old black things, why don't you go away and *wash!*

Jokes can bring a blessing to the inexorability of pain?

Or how is suffering to be understood by Christians in a world that is said to have been redeemed by Christ? You partake of Christ's suffering? You are thus co-purveyors of redemption? But these are words: what is the experience.

There is something mysterious, seldom admitted, about humans' relationship with pain. People seek it out, make spiritual use of it – on high mountains, in arctic regions, on rough seas. Through confrontation with hardship they say they experience meaning – for themselves; with regard to the world. And for this, pain seems to be not incidental but a condition. Some mothers after childbirth say they would not have foregone the pain. And this does not seem unnatural.

People who wished to feel holy used to flagellate themselves. Then the word 'masochism' was discovered, and such practices became 'kinky.' But by then much of religion had begun to be called kinky; though not the climbing of high mountains.

I found no spirituality while on traction – except perhaps through the routine of the four-hour gaps between my shots of morphine. The first hour was bliss, the second not too bad, the third full of anxiety, then the fourth hell – in which one seemed to be suspended only just above the flames. And so one prayed, yes; what else was there to do? And by this perhaps learned something about requirements of the human condition.

But I did continue to feel strangely that I had not been hard-done-by by my condition. I ruminated on what had been happening over the last months and even years. It seemed that the actors in what I came to see as comedy – me, Natalie, her husband – had all been at the mercy of archetypal forces which we both raged against and at the same time welcomed. At first it had seemed that Natalie and I were puppets whose strings were pulled by her husband; then we took advantage of this, and it seemed he was as helpless as we. Then I had felt us all as victims of some juggernaut; but were we not also worshippers of the chances and opportunities it provided? There had been a sense of exhilaration as well as of approaching doom; had this been a pattern in the Gospels? But what of the Spirit that should come after?

What did seem to offer a sense of blessing as a result of my accident was that Rosemary came down from her fastness in the Isle of Man and stayed with friends nearby from where she could visit me. And this she did, each day, like an indubitable angel. At the start of the visiting hour I would watch for her to come through the door and I would say – I will never forget this! I will now always be true to you! She might look doubtful. And I could hardly blame her.

Before long I did begin to worry, yes, about Natalie: what had happened to her; what would become of her if her husband threw her out again or had not taken her back; would she have any means by which to live? A mutual friend came down to see me and I asked him – Can you just see if she's all right? He said – Oh don't worry about her, she's gone to St Tropez. I said – St Tropez! He said – I think she's been lent a studio there, and is painting. I thought – Now surely I'm not going to be like Proust's all-too-human hero who does not worry much about his girlfriend when he thinks she may be sad, but becomes wildly jealous when he hears she may be happy. And then – Oh Rosemary, I'm so sorry! Could we not try to make a go of it again?

When my bones had been set and the time came for me to be transferred to a hospital near to my home in London, the ambulance man who accompanied me on a stretcher on the train was one of the men who had extracted me from the car at the time of the accident. He said – I'm glad to see you; we were afraid you might not survive! I said – Why? He said – Well, three things could have killed you: first just the shock of so many of your bones being broken; secondly, the chances of the jagged end of your femur cutting into a major artery and you bleeding to death; but mainly the fact that the marrow of this bone was so exposed that you were likely to pick up a lethal infection very quickly. I said – And what would have prevented that? He said – Well, it was as if you had already had a shot of antibiotics before we got to you. I then remembered – That morning, I had had to go to my dentist with an abscess under a tooth and he had prescribed a course of antibiotic tablets, which I had begun to take. I can't remember whether or not I told this to the ambulance man; it's difficult for anyone to take on board such a story – even oneself.

In London I went to the Royal Free Hospital in Hampstead to be near my home; there I continued to mend. And here at last Natalie came to visit me. She seemed bursting with health and vigour; she said she had been lent a studio in St Tropez, yes, so she had abandoned her piano and dedicated herself to painting. I found it possible not to ask too many questions. I began to think – As soon as I can walk, all things may be possible!

After a time I was carried still on a stretcher to my home in Church Row. But there my faithful housekeeper June was on the point of having a baby. So Rosemary said that for the time being she would take me in at the Isle of Man. So then I was thinking again – Might it not be best, yes, after all, for me to settle in again with Rosemary, if this seems to be the way that things are working out.

There was a ruined cottage by Rosemary's land at the northernmost tip of the Isle of Man which I had explored when I had been staying in earlier holidays. It was a beautiful, isolated somewhat haunted place, surrounded by bones. The previous occupant had been a hermit and was said to have lived by killing and eating sheep and not burying their remains. I began to think I might buy the place and do it up and move there when my own bones were mended; surely Rosemary and I could come to this odd sort of accommodation? I could become a hermit; which was the only condition, I now began to imagine, in which an orderly life might be possible.

So I was flown up to the Isle of Man still on a stretcher. And I thought, did I, that fate might be back in my hands?

I was still bedridden but recovering quietly in Rosemary's spare room when my old friend Aelred, now teaching at the theological college for Africans in Cape Province (this was just before he met Steve Biko) came to England on leave and wrote to say he must pay me a visit. Rosemary had never got on with Aelred; she sensed correctly that he saw her as a rival. His previous leave from South Africa had coincided with my early days with Natalie: he had met her and they had got on well together – he encouraged her to read bits of the New Testament, which she said were an eye-opener. But then should not he, as a priest, have been more critical of my infidelity? Now, in the Isle of Man, Rosemary said she did not want him to stay in the house. I could understand this; but said – What harm can he do? Surely I cannot refuse to see my oldest friend! And so it was agreed that we would put him up in the local hotel, and he could come out to see me in a taxi.

So Aelred came, and he sat by my bed in Rosemary's upstairs room; and without much further ado he began to recount to me how in London he had gone to see Natalie; and she was yes, going back, or had already gone back, to her husband, so I needn't worry about that. And she was in tremendously good spirits because she had had a wonderful summer in St Tropez being involved in a love-affair with a most marvellous Frenchman. By this time I was having a sort of fit. There is a scene in the opera *Otello* when Iago, having imbued Othello with jealousy, watches with satisfaction as he writhes on the floor. And I had thought that this might be played as farce! And now here I was on my back like a half-squashed beetle with my arms and legs waving in the air. Aelred affected not to understand what was happening. He said 'I thought you would want to hear her news.' I think quite a large part of my distress was that my oldest friend, my early guide to Christianity, was behaving with such callousness when I was evidently still so frail. He went down to Rosemary to ask her what was the matter. She got him a taxi to go back to his hotel.

In later years Aelred explained that while teaching theology in South Africa he had got out the way of understanding the ways of the wicked world; my reaction to his news had bewildered and even disgusted him. And I suppose it disgusted me: I had felt so superior to Proust's hero! But I had also become accustomed to relying on brethren of the Community for reassurance; so this was a double near-knock-out blow. But then – if Aelred was now behaving like Mephistopheles, might not his machinations in the end engender good? Surely what I had to accept now was that it was my own devils I had to confront; and not to dream of destiny being taken out of my hands. And for this I would have to get fit; and not languish in the feebleness of having been smashed up in a car crash.

And Aelred returned to South Arica, where he was soon to meet Steve Biko.

- 16 -

Now that it seemed I was on my own – with no help in sight from old friends, old loved ones; surely now even from super-loyal Rosemary, who was the person with most right to be disgusted with what had been going on – in this situation it seemed indeed vital to become mobile as soon as possible. And in this respect had I not been greatly favoured? I had been told I might well be dead, might never walk on two legs again, might lose the use of my right arm. And now here I was learning to stump up and down in the lanes of the Isle of Man on crutches – though not usual crutches, because the break in my forearm meant that no weight could be put on that hand, so one crutch had to be horizontal at the place where weight could be put on the elbow, with the forearm resting along it. I felt my energy coming back, I suppose nourished by rage – but rage mainly against myself, for having for so long let myself be blown about like chaff. Watching and listening was all very well; but did not the time come for one to be like those stern Christian warrior-saints with their bright armour and steady gaze whom I had once thought irrelevant? I now felt the necessity to outflank my radiant Natalie and her demon lover: why had she never been to see me when I was lying at death's door? Because I had told her I never wanted to see her again? Oh all right! But might she not have known that this sort of thing was rubbish? But no more recriminations! On to Jerusalem!

With me in this mood my faithful Rosemary was understandably only too glad to be rid of me: she had never in fact given much encouragement to the idea of our getting back together. After a few weeks I was well enough to get a taxi to the Isle of Man airport; I arrived in London still on my ungainly crutches but at least with some mobility. I telephoned Natalie and she agreed to have lunch with me. She said she was on the point, yes, of moving back with her husband, so I needn't worry about her and the children. At lunch I said I would marry her. I did not think this was only hysteria; it had never been said before, and it had struck me that this might be why our to-and-fro dragged on so interminably. She now looked somewhat disconcerted. I remember thinking – So now, thank goodness, this may be the beginning of the end! She said nothing. I settled in again in my beautiful house in Hampstead where my faithful housekeeper June and her new baby were in the basement.

I wondered – Might one even learn to act deliberately paradoxically?

During the previous two years, following the success of the film of *Accident*, I had been working on and off with Joseph Losey on a script for a film of my novel *Impossible Object*. The novel had been on the short list for the first Booker Prize in 1969, but had been considered too experimental. Losey had become enthusiastic about the book and now my script, though he saw it might be difficult to raise money for a film. The script echoed the enigmas of the book: one of these being – no one ever quite does get the best of both worlds, but if one has a shot at this one might, in spite of potential or even actual catastrophe, achieve – what? Could one ever quite say? What life was meant to be? At least lively?

I had kept in touch with Losey while I was out of action from my accident, but any film of *Impossible Object* still awaited funding. Then when I was back in London Losey telephoned to say that he had a contract to make a film about the assassination of Trotsky, but he had not yet been able to get a decent script for it. The obvious writers he had tried had littered their scripts with unactable Marxist jargon. Now that I was back in London but still laid up, would I like to have a go at it? I was the least politically-minded writer that he knew, he said, so I should at least avoid the jargon. But did I know anything about Trotsky?

I said that I had read and much admired his autobiography, so yes, I would like to have a go. And it seemed to me anyway that Trotsky was not an orthodox Marxist, or why should Stalin have wanted to assassinate him? So I was offered a contract to write a script; a proviso being that a first draft would have to be done and looked at within three weeks, or Losey might lose the stars who had provisionally committed themselves to the project and who were vital to the funding. So I sat up in bed and read Isaac Deutscher's three-volume biography of Trotsky by night, and by day I wrote several pages of script; and every evening a huge American car would arrive and take my pages away for perusal. And at the end of three weeks Losey told me that he, the Hollywood producer Joseph Shaftel, and Alain Delon – the vital star who was to play the part of the assassin – all liked the script, and so the whole project was under way.

I thought – This is the sort of thing that happens to knights in armour who set off for Jerusalem?

Most writers dream of a chance to work in films. I had needed a change anyway from my *Impossible Object* type novels. (*Natalie Natalia* had also been taken up with the difficult years with Natalie, the title expressive of her dual nature of impossible sprite and angel.) I had had high hopes of my *Impossible Object* script; but now with the Trotsky project there were assured contracts and funding. So if this was not Jerusalem, it seemed to me a Hollywood version of it.

Losey and I worked together to expand and elaborate my script. The story takes place when Trotsky is an old man in Mexico City with Stalinist agents pursuing him to kill him. Political background had to be put into the script to explain who Trotsky was and why Stalin wanted to kill him. It seemed that the best way to do this was by flashbacks to the time of the Russian Revolution when Trotsky had been Lenin's right-hand-man; then Lenin had died and Stalin had taken over. These scenes were worked out carefully – to be shot in grainy black and white as if they were from contemporary newsreels. Losey and I drank whisky in the evenings; he reminisced about the time when he had been a Stalinist in America in the thirties and had been in touch with contacts in Russia. I did not talk about my present personal preoccupations; Losey had met Natalie while making the film of *Accident* and had thought her beautiful and had wanted to find a small part in the film for her; but then he and she had quarrelled when we had all happened to bump into one another on a trip to Venice. Losey had warned me that she was 'dangerous.' I had thought – How true! But now in the course of my doing the Trotsky script Natalie and I were seeing each other again, though nothing more was ever said about marriage. Perhaps she was now influenced by my having become preoccupied elsewhere; perhaps her husband had gone off with yet another woman. Or just – things once more seemed to have taken over their own organisation.

The time came when the organisation of the Trotsky film moved from London to Rome, where there were studios which could be used for some of the interior shots. I was needed for possible further re-writes on the script, so I was flown out first class and put up in a five-star hotel. Losey had met Rosemary in London when she had been staying with me for some occasion to do with the children's schools. He had taken to Rosemary as clearly as he had not taken to Natalie; he had said to her – Why not come to Rome? But Rosemary had been dismayed by the prospect of being a token film-wife with nothing to do but sit around in Rome: so she had said No. And then when I was there with the film people myself now with nothing much to do (my script was being picked over by art-director, production manager, and so on) it transpired – oh Lord! – that Natalie and her children were once more virtually homeless in London, her husband apparently this time having proposed marriage to at least two other women. And so Natalie and the children were once more in urgent need of somewhere to go. So I asked the film finance people if they would swap my room in the five-star hotel for two rooms in a beautiful but much cheaper hotel of which both Natalie and I knew to one side of the Piazza Navona near where Losey had his apartment. Losey said – She's pursuing you! I said – Well Rosemary wouldn't come. I was thinking – however absurdly – But perhaps now I am a bit more in control of my fate.

So Natalie and her children came and we moved into two beautiful rooms whose balconies seemed to be the roof of a neighbouring church; and we went sightseeing, because my work as a scriptwriter seemed to be done. There came a time when Richard Burton and Elizabeth Taylor were said to be due to call in on their yacht at Ostia, the port of Rome; and I was asked to be on call when this occurred, because Losey had his eye on Richard Burton to play the part of Trotsky, and I might be needed to add my weight, such as it was, to Burton's enrolment. Natalie and I and the children had planned to go that day to see a rarely visited church outside the city walls; I said that she and the children could go, but I would have to stay. Natalie was unimpressed by film celebrities unless they were stars of her favourite films. I said – But you don't understand; this is like being summoned to greet King Solomon and the Queen of Sheba! She said – I thought you said they were Richard Burton and Elizabeth Taylor. So I went to look at the rare Romanesque church; and never did get to meet Elizabeth Taylor.

I tried to make up later for my lack of commitment by volunteering to go out at my own expense to Mexico City when filming began there. I had been told that a bunch of Mexican Trotskyites had got hold of my script and were objecting to the contents of a work which, they had realised, had been written by a Mosley (i.e., 'fascist') and was being directed by an ex-Stalinist. Some of the outdoor sets had begun to be picketed. When I reached Mexico City I told Losey that I would go and talk to the Trotskyites. Losey was sceptical about this: he said 'But the point of you is that you are a political innocent!' I said 'Exactly.' So I went off by taxi one evening to an address in Coyoacán – the suburb where Trotsky's house was in which he had been murdered – and there I found a group of stern middle-aged Trotskyites sitting round a table. We argued for a time in guarded but hostile English about whether or not my script conveyed an acceptable portrait of Trotsky's politics; then I said 'Well tell me exactly what you think I have omitted and should not have done.' They conferred among themselves; then said 'Equal pay for blue-collar and white-collar workers.' I said 'You really think I should get Trotsky, an old man in Mexico in 1940, suddenly exclaiming – ' "Equal pay for blue-collar and white-collar workers!?" ' After a time they laughed; then someone produced a bottle of Mexican brandy; and then for an hour or so we had what I might call an appropriate political conversation, because we got drunk. When I got back to the hotel I found Losey waiting up for me like an anxious parent. He said 'We thought you might have been murdered!' I was recalling – At the time of the Russian Revolution, Trotsky said that everyone except the Bolsheviks were drunk.

My next involvement with the film was when the editing had moved to Paris and I heard on some grapevine that Losey was cutting all the flashback scenes from Leninist and Stalinist days; this would leave the politics and indeed Trotsky's presence in Mexico unexplained, and so would render the film unintelligible. When I telephoned to Losey he at first didn't want to talk; then just said that the flashbacks had proved to be unworkable in cinematic terms. I went to see him in Paris; there was a new entourage around him – brisk and bossy Frenchmen who I took to be Stalinists, and who were not susceptible to charm as the Mexican Trotskyites had been. And Losey was now putting blame for the changes on inadequacies in my script. Much later, when I was on reasonably good terms with him again, he said that when he was in Paris he had been telephoned from Prague by one of his old Stalinist 'contacts' of the 1930s, who had said to him 'Joe, what's all this about a film of Trotsky? We're watching you!'

I went to the producer, Joseph Shaftel, and said that what Losey insisted on cutting from the script would ruin the film. He said there was nothing he could do about this, because Losey had artistic control. But if I objected to what was happening then he, Shaftel, would commission me here and now to write a 'book of the film.' However it would have to be done in six weeks in order to be out in time for the premier of the film. I said 'No one can write a book about Trotsky in six weeks!' He said 'But you haven't asked what money I'm offering you!' I was about to say – Oh I don't really have to worry about that. But I said 'How much?' And when he told me I said 'All right I'll do it!'

It wasn't a bad little book. It was dismissed as irrelevant by some home-grown Trotskyites, but I found myself invited and welcomed to some Workers' Revolutionary parties.

My dispute with Losey – he had written to me to try to stop me doing the book – meant that it was no longer feasible for him to try to set up a film from my *Impossible Object* script. But the success of the film of *Accident,* and now optimistic rumours of the forthcoming *Trotsky,* had made my name known as a writer in the film world. And then while the editing of *Trotsky* was being further delayed by various disputes, a big-name director from Hollywood, John Frankenheimer, arrived in London. He had recently made excellent big-budget films such as *The Manchurian Candidate* and *Seven Days in May,* and had come to Europe on the look-out for a script from which he could make an unmistakably 'art' movie. My agent Anthony Jones heard of this, and sent him my *Impossible Object* script, saying – This is the art-movie script to end all art-movie scripts. I was summoned to have breakfast with Frankenheimer in his suite at the Connaught Hotel. He was a tall youngish man, fierce and energetic. He said – I want you to explain to me not the story, such as it is, but why you wrote it like that. I said – For most of the time people are acting a part, doing a spiel; they both know this and don't. Occasionally – perhaps when in love – people want to cut out the play-acting and say, and be, what is true; but how can they do this or know it? The script tries to differentiate between when people are doing a spiel, acting, and when they are trying to say what is true. It even asks the question – If you know you are acting, then is what you're doing in some sense true? And so on. Frankenheimer paced up and down, occasionally pausing to glare at me. Breakfast was wheeled in and out, scarcely touched. When I had run out of steam Frankenheimer just faced me and said 'I'll do it!' And soon he was going off to raise the necessary several million dollars and enrol good stars.

In London Frankenheimer had met Natalie and had taken to her as much as Losey had not. Later he wanted Natalie and me to move to Paris where he would be setting up the film with French-Canadian money;

he said he would find an apartment for us on the Île de la Cité. We did stay in Paris for a while; but I began to foresee disasters such as there had been with the Trotsky film. When in due course there began to be readings of the script and rehearsals, it became apparent that neither Frankenheimer nor most of the actors had taken on board much of the idea of the difference between what is acting and what is not. Or perhaps it is impossible for even expert actors to act what is not acting.

And just then there was the premier of *Trotsky* in Paris, which Natalie and I attended; and although I was impressed with what Losey had done with what was left of the script, the whole thing made little sense – who was this old man blathering on in Mexico City – and the film got mostly bad notices in the papers. Frankenheimer took note of these. And then concurrently there was a savagely hostile review by Philip Toynbee in the *Observer* of my written-in-six-weeks Trotsky book, saying – How could I, a spoilt and decadent Englishman, have the cheek to write about some of the greatest affairs of the twentieth century and treat them with such lack of portentousness? So having been a flavour-of-the-month as it were in the film world I became overnight something of a pariah; and it was becoming clear that any views I expressed about the making of the film of *Impossible Object* would carry as little weight as had my views about *Trotsky*. So Frankenheimer and I fell out. I think he was also disappointed by Natalie deciding to leave Paris and return to London in order to be on hand for her children who were at school. And so Natalie and I retreated to Hampstead, and I began to try to put what I had been wanting to portray in my scripts into a form in which no one would be able to ignore or pervert this. That is, I would write a play (I thought I would call it 'play for not acting') in which it would be unavoidably explicit about when the characters were putting over a 'line' and when they were trying to be 'true.' And the ability to become aware of this sort of thing, the play would suggest, was most urgently required by humans.

My last meeting with Frankenheimer was when Natalie and I paused in Paris on our way to a walking tour in the Black Forest with her and my two younger children. This was Easter 1972, and it was very cold, and snowing heavily. I joked to Frankenheimer – Perhaps our walk in the Black Forest will be like the last story of *Impossible Object* in which one of the children, as a result of the parents' irresponsible behaviour, dies. I don't think he thought this funny. While in Paris we watched one of the scenes of the film being shot with Alan Bates and Dominique Sanda as the lovers. It seemed that she at least might be getting the style right, because to her English was anyway a foreign language.

We survived the Black Forest walking tour. But it seemed that with all of us the *commedia dell'arte* style was running out of steam. It was as if Natalie and I as performers were getting exhausted, and were longing for the curtain to come down, and for us to go somewhere which might be called home.

Some time previously I had written the draft of a conventional play in which passengers on a plane in the 1950s are stranded at a stop-over airport in the Atlantic. One of their number is a manacled victim/prisoner being taken (it becomes apparent) by armed guards back behind the iron curtain – to a gulag? to be shot? And the other passengers wonder whether they should do anything to try to rescue him. This play had been bought by independent television; but at the last moment had been scotched. One of the characters was an arrogant ex-SS officer also returning from exile; he is contemptuous of the others for their concern and yet helplessness; he sets about freeing the prisoner himself, and in doing so gets shot. He was an unpleasant and suicidal man, but perhaps too much like a hero.

I thought I should now try to write a play about people being stranded in, as it were, the airport of their minds; could any of them act any differently from the effects of their conditioning? This was the play that might be called *Play for Not Acting*.

But having got out of films, how on earth was I to get out of what seemed to be my own conditioning – that which landed me in an apparently endless cycle of convoluted personal relationships and traps and dilemmas, however much I might try to see these as farce?

In the summer after the walking tour in the Black Forest I took a house by the sea in Majorca which was large enough to accommodate anyone of whatever family chose to join me there. Natalie still had the use of my old London flat, and was choosing to stay there to be close to her children's schools. Rosemary and my younger children were based mainly in the Isle of Man; our two older children were at university and came and went with their friends to and from Church Row. My way of dealing with our absurd predicaments seemed to be to keep freedom of movement open so as not to feel trapped; and then there might be chances for things to develop as it were off-stage. I remember little of the details of this time; though there was a general impression of an end-game being played.

To the house in Majorca I took a huge number of books from which I hoped to garner some philosophical background to the ideas about acting or not acting that were floating about in my mind. I drove out to Majorca with my two younger children, Robert and Clare, and there we each lay in different corners of a flat roof and sunbathed and devoured books. I read Karl Popper, Gregory Bateson, Suzanne Langer, R. D. Laing. Clare, aged eleven, got hold of the latter's *The Divided Self* and said – I didn't know other families were like ours! After a time it was Rosemary who came out to join us; she had been somewhat ill in the Isle of Man and needed a holiday. We were all quiet and respectful. I thought – Yes, if there are no histrionics, one is not trapped.

But how would one know if anything was going on off-stage?

Some time the following winter Natalie and her son returned to Church Row. In the spring Rosemary was staying with friends in the south of France where Clare was for a term learning French. When in the summer I had become fit enough to drive after my accident I had celebrated by buying a second-hand Mercedes in which I whizzed to-and-fro between Hampstead and the South of France. This sort of life left little time for introspective histrionics; but there was little stillness in which to watch and listen for anything going on off-stage. Sooner or later – such an outcome once more seemed inevitable – I went to a party in Oxford and there got drunk and on the way home overturned my beautiful car on a corner. I stepped out unharmed, and was in fact directing traffic when police arrived. I told them – 'It's funny, I once wrote a story in which there was an accident just like this!' I spent the night in a cell, and was banned for driving for a year. So I bought a bicycle and free-wheeled happily down the hills from Hampstead, but had to push the bike much of the way up again. By this time Natalie, still with me in Hampstead, was going to a psychoanalyst four or five times a week. Analysis had hitherto played no part in my life. I had read most of Jung and bits of Freud; but this had been for intellectual exercise.

Then there came an evening when my Natalie's analyst rang me to inquire if she had returned home safely. Natalie had apparently left her session in a state of distress; and she, the analyst, was anxious. I said yes, Natalie had arrived home in a state apparently not much more stressed than usual. But I asked – Could I possibly come and talk to her, the analyst, because I might learn things about Natalie that might explain and even alleviate some of the continuing absurdity of our situation. And she said Yes.

So I went to Natalie's analyst and she was a pleasant middle-aged woman. She said that it was unethical for her to talk much to me because Natalie was her patient. But she had agreed to see me because she could fix me up with another analyst, a friend of hers, and he and I could talk freely. My first reaction was – But I don't need an analyst! But this seemed absurd. And then Natalie's analyst said – You must surely see that your problem is not to try to understand your girlfriend's problem, but to understand and deal with your own. I thought of saying – But I know my problem! But this seemed untrue. Or rather – my problem was that I knew I was stuck with my problem. So I said – Yes, I see that.

So the next day Natalie's analyst telephoned to say that she had fixed an appointment for me to see her friend the other analyst. I thought – Well that is extraordinarily kind! Even though they must see me as a basket case. So I went off to my appointment with the other analyst, Michael Fordham, whom I knew to be (and was thus impressed) one of the editors of Jung's collected works. He was a quiet, confident man, who said immediately that he must make it plain that he was so booked up that he could only see me just this once for a consultation, during which however we could see what might be a next move. We sat facing each other; and I poured out all the rigmarole, the tos-and-fros, of my life with Natalie and Rosemary. I said I realised it was all a bit of a farce, yes; but that was what life was like, no? He listened impassively; and then at the end of my effusion just said 'You're a greedy baby.' I thought – Well, that's a remarkable thing to say! Should I feel insulted? But after a moment I said 'Anyway, what's wrong with a greedy baby?' And he said 'I have not said there's anything wrong with a greedy baby.' And I thought – That's even more remarkable! I said 'I see.' He said 'Do you?' But now my fifty minutes were up, and he was showing me to the door. With his hand on the handle he said 'I could see you four times a week if you like' and I said 'Yes, I would like, thank you.' And that is how I became involved in what might be called the anti-farce of analysis.

*

One reason I suppose why I had been slow personally to take on board the claims of psychoanalysis was that I had imagined that any such process would get hung up on the matter of my father – of his reputation for being such a demon; of my having been told when I was ten or eleven that he was responsible for my mother's death. And I did not want to get hung up in trying to explain how this sort of accusation had tended to make me sympathetic to my father. But now – if I were a 'greedy baby' – what could this have to do with my father?

And indeed one of the stories that emerged as I trundled down the hill four times a week on my bicycle was one that had been told me more than once by my Nanny. She had been a great teller of stories from her experience and memories, and would use this talent to amuse us children. This particular story that I now found myself recounting to Dr Fordham was about how my mother, just after my birth, had found that she could not breast-feed me; and so she had hired a wet-nurse – this being a practice not uncommon at the time amongst families who could afford it. So I had dangled from one of the breasts of this well-endowed person while her own newly-born baby, I suppose, dangled from the other. And my mother, because it was now getting on towards August, went off with my father for their annual summer holiday to Venice – this being another custom in the upper-class course of things which would conventionally take precedence over a baby's difficulty with food. So Nanny and I and the wet-nurse and her baby had gone to Frinton-on-Sea, in Essex; a favoured resort for upper-class children and their minders while their parents were elsewhere. But at Frinton my feeding and my health did not improve. According to Nanny (and she sent letters about this to my mother which I later came across) I vomited the milk provided by the wet-nurse; I was increasingly undernourished and seemed to be wasting away. Eventually Nanny felt she had to take matters into her own hands, and hired a car to take me to a specialist child-doctor in London whom we knew – having to borrow the cost from the taxi-owner because my mother had not left her with enough money for emergencies. The child-doctor said that I was suffering from starvation: Nanny must ensure that I had nothing more to do with the wet-nurse, and should begin to feed me forthwith with the new-on-the-market Cow-and-Gate powdered milk, of which he would give her a supply to start her off. So Nanny went back to Frinton and got rid of the wet-nurse; and after she had gone, Nanny found a crate of empty gin-bottles under her bed. This was the punch-line of Nanny's story. She told it as a funny story; as I did, years later, to my analyst. He said 'Why are you laughing?' I said 'I don't know.' He said 'But this is a terrible story!' I thought – And it's one about not my father but my mother, who was supposed to have been such a martyred saint!

As my analysis burrowed away it was this sort of realisation that emerged from the woodwork: my father as a father had been no worse than most fathers of his class and generation; but my mother – well she was of her class and generation too, but she had subjugated everything to the needs of her husband (I interposed – But they quarrelled!). Dr Fordham went on – And here you are now with a bad stammer, having been poisoned through the mouth and left gasping for air during the first months of your life; and you are still having to go round searching for sustenance, for love, like a cat scavenging beneath dustbin-lids in alleys. (I thought – What, my beautiful Natalie, my Mary, dustbins in alleys? Well surely this might be taken as funny!) But curiously, wondrously, like a ghost coming through woodwork, it did make some sort of sense, yes.

All right, but what could be done about it now? Was not one's nature moulded?

Dr Fordham seemed to suggest – Just carry on whizzing down Hampstead hill four times a week on your bike. And see what happens.

I thought – And seeing if one can pedal a little further back up the hill each time without dismounting?

I had in fact praised Freud and Jung some seven years ago in my book *Experience and Religion,* which had signalled my distancing from conventional religion. I had called them modern religious prophets, because they had faith that by easing shut-away memories out of the mouldering junk-cupboard of the mind – just by exposing them as it were to light and air – it might happen that a person became aware of the underlying truth of things, and an exorcism of falsity might be effected. And so (I had argued) did this not assume the natural existence of an unseen force for health, for good, if only it was given by humans the chance to operate? And why should not this be the sort of force which Christians referred to when they spoke – if they ever did get round to mentioning it – of a Ghost, or Spirit?

Anyway my analysis was opening up new avenues of discovery and fascination, and for a time I was eager to get on my bike for another session. And then Natalie's husband suddenly and unexpectedly died; and this seemed to break whatever had been the yo-yo string on which it seemed for so long we had all depended. Dr Fordham said – I suppose you and your girl are now going to start blaming yourselves. I wondered – You mean, we shouldn't? But anyway, more and more ties binding us did seem to be unravelling; and Natalie and her children, in mourning, went once more to live in my old flat. And I on my own – perhaps with some guilt, but also with a sense that the jaws of our trap might be opening – could get on with writing my play.

I had been finding it difficult to talk about this to Fordham – about the difference between acting and not acting, and might it be not-acting if one knew that one was acting? Also the business of something happening, or not, off-stage. Fordham said 'You like tying yourself in knots.' I said 'I think people are in knots, and they don't like untying themselves.'

I wondered – Perhaps he doesn't like this because it might be a sort of self-analysis?

Then there came a day when I whizzed down the hill with more abandon than usual because I had a new and dramatic story to tell my analyst about what had happened to me the evening before. And when I had finished holding forth – perhaps in unusually enthusiastic style – Fordham just said – 'You have now found your good breast!'

Which in analytical terms meant, did it, that I might no longer have to scavenge under dustbin-lids in alleys?

What had happened the evening before was that I had been asked by a couple with whom I was friends to make up a four to go to the theatre – the fourth being a friend of theirs who was on her own having recently left her husband. So there was a bit of match-making going on, was there? Well, so be it. The play, or show, was *The Rocky Horror Show*. The person I was being paired with arrived late. In the half-dark I looked along the row and saw – someone indubitably beautiful, yes; and somehow at once both waifish and formidable. I thought – Well that's all right! Then afterwards when we were all in her car and going to have supper in her house near Shepherd's Bush, I embarked on a somewhat rambling spiel about why I thought *The Rocky Horror Show* so awful. I was still banging on about this when we arrived at her house and had settled into the kitchen, and she had her back to us by the stove. She had hardly yet spoken. Then when I had at last done with my act, she just said 'I've never heard such rubbish in all my life!'

I thought – Well that, here and now, both on and off-stage, is remarkable!

(Later, after I had heard Dr Fordham's comment on the full story, I wondered – Is what he calls a good breast that which enables one to distinguish between what is an act and what is not –

– to be able to choose, that is, what is true rather than what is not?)

Supper had been somewhat stilted. Our mutual friends must have thought their matchmaking plans a disaster. Then when we were all leaving to go our different ways, I paused by our hostess's front door where there was a photograph on a shelf of a beautiful one-year-old boy. I said 'Is he yours?' She said 'Yes.' I said 'It makes one want to start all over again!' The others were out in the street. She murmured 'You don't have to go.' I said 'Ah, one never quite knows!' So I stayed; and there was the discovery of what anyone indeed might call good breast.

Her one proviso was that I had to be out by half past six in the morning, because after that her one-year-old son, Jonathan, was liable to appear from upstairs with his Filipino minder. So at six her alarm went off and I struggled up, and she said 'Leave your telephone number on the blotter by the bed.' So I wrote *Nicholas Mosley* and my Hampstead number, and groped my way towards the door. There was a shout of 'Oi!' from the bed. She had propped herself up and was looking at the blotter. She said 'I thought you were called something different.' So I tottered back and wrote *Ravensdale* with a flourish, and went on to the door. She said 'That's better.' Then she rolled over and went back to sleep.

Walking home in the clear light of dawn I thought – In God's name, barriers do seem to be coming down between what is on and what is off-stage!

The next evening she came to have dinner with me in Church Row, where the drawing room was festooned with Rosemary's old-master paintings. She made no comment about these. But on the landing just outside there was a cuckoo-clock which I had bought and carried home in my rucksack on the walking-tour with Natalie in the Black Forest. My new friend and I were reclining on the sofa when this clock went 'Cuckoo! Cuckoo!' eleven times. She looked up briefly and said 'That cuckoo clock will have to go.'

I thought – You mean, love and truth are joined, when one knows oneself to be both on and off-stage.

And soon my new friend, who happened to be called Verity, was moving into Church Row. And my faithful housekeeper June was leaving, but Verity put such a glowing testimonial for her in the *Lady* magazine that she was almost immediately off to an even better-sounding housekeeping job in the country.

And I was thinking – You mean, love may not be really a fantasy, a sickness, an obsession, a *commedia* –

– but an expression of the way in which the world works, can truly work, if one gets through all the rigmarole with trust?

- 18 -

It is my hope that the last third of this book may be seen as an attempt to get past experience as tragedy or farce, and to see it as a journey in which impossible paradoxes such as freedom and commitment, fidelity and exploration, can be appreciated as possible objects in an eternal landscape.

Marriages are usually seen as either routinely straightforward or a disaster. Tolstoy, in the opening sentences of *Anna Karenina*, suggests that there is nothing distinctive about happy marriages, and thus they are too boring to be written about. But in what sense are marriages happy if they are boring? Happiness is either a dream; or that which you have to work hard and with skill for.

To get back into Eden, it has been said, one has to go right round the world and in by the back way. One naturally does not exactly get there: but it is the journey – on one's own or perhaps more hazardously but responsibly two-by-two – that may have done what God requires.

It was my hope that the last third of this book might be seen as an account of a good marriage – one that had to be, and was, worked at and fought for. Love involves two people aiming to occupy the same space at the same time; and thus inevitably is sometimes like war. Things have to be risked, entrusted to luck, if one is to succeed – as in war. There can be near disaster, near despair; but there either is or is not trust. And so one either does or does not come through.

Verity and I were both what a psychiatrist has called 'damaged creatures.' But still, people do come through.

Verity's family on her father's side came to England from New Zealand in the early nineteen hundreds. During the Second World War her father was an industrialist owning and running a factory making optical instruments for armaments. He was an expert sailor, and became a leading member of the Royal Yacht Squadron. When Verity was a teenager her parents retired to become pillars of local society in Hampshire.

When I was introduced to Verity's mother – at tea in Verity's house in Shepherd's Bush – she would at first hardly speak to me; she caressed an elegant whippet on her lap. Her comment to Verity afterwards was – 'He's so old.'

When Verity took me for the weekend to her parent's house in Hampshire I was warned by her brother-in-law – who happened to be the film producer who had commissioned me to write a script about the pop concert on the way to which I had had my car crash – 'Watch out for her father, he's hostile to anyone who he sees as a prospective son-in-law.' And then at dinner, after the ladies had left the gentlemen to their port, Verity's father duly and bluntly contradicted everything I said. So I thought I'd better get it over with, and told him he was being rude. He walked out of the room. When I joined the ladies in the drawing room I said to Verity's mother that I had had a row with her husband and was sorry; whereupon she came over and kissed me on the cheek. After that her husband reappeared and we all seemed to get on well together.

So indeed – A tricky background here!

Verity's elder sister and her husband the film producer came to have dinner at Church Row. I sat next to the sister and she said to me out of the blue – 'You may think you'll get Verity, but you'll never take her away from her mother!' I said 'You shouldn't say things like that!' She walked out of the room. Her husband smiled at me from across the table.

Tricky, yes. But a challenge!

Soon after Verity's and my first meeting, which had seemed to me so romantic and momentous, Verity sat me down and said that she wanted to tell me one or two things about her previous life. (She was thirty-one). She had run away from school, never passed an exam, trained for a time as a ballet dancer; then when her parents thought she was attending a dress-making school in London, she had allowed them to think this and went partying with a group of boyfriends at Oxford. Later she got herself jobs in London – first behind the front desk at the auctioneers Christie's; then as a fashion-buyer at Harvey Nichols. Her considerable success at these jobs seemed to be due both to her efficiency, and to clients bringing their business to these places in order to ask her out to lunch. She was, and is, extraordinarily beautiful.

Sooner or later she was under the wing of a rich and powerful older man who took her to stay in his houses in Cowes and Switzerland; then by private plane to his island in the Bahamas. At Cowes he was a member of the Royal Yacht Squadron, along with Verity's father. Her parents, who had tried to keep a puritanical eye on any younger pursuer, appeared not to notice this notable admirer.

And then Verity told me, looking me straight in the eye, how this elderly fellow, in order as it were to keep himself going, had liked to film her in certain fanciful situations – not too good, not too bad – no?

I wondered – Why is she telling me this? Because she wants to see if I will flee or take up the challenge? Because she knows such boldness, and indeed such stories, can, if the listener is bold too, be something of a turn-on?

Quite like the challenges of war.

Verity had married her first husband, whom she had loved, partly in order to get out of her evidently dead-end relationship with the older man. She and her husband had had their son Jonathan, then they had separated, amicably, but when I met Verity they were not yet divorced.

Rosemary and I were separated, but had not talked of divorce. We had given each other chances to get back together, but this had not happened. Natalie, since the death of her husband, had stayed in my old flat with her children. After a time there were indications that she had a new lover. I wondered if I might again have an Othello-type fit; but surely I had got over this by now; had learnt that such pointless tendencies were better seen as farce. So I managed – What the hell! And to signify responsibly the end of our long relationship, I set about handing over to Natalie the lease of my flat.

My analyst, Dr Fordham, seemed to have seen it as one of his tasks from the beginning of my analysis to mastermind the end of my affair with Natalie; also to see that I did not now mess up my relationship with Verity. It turned out that he was a friend and colleague of the analyst that Verity had for some time been going to, Dr Tom Main; and it was now as if the two of them saw themselves in the role of parents making sure of a shotgun wedding. When Verity told Dr Main of her and my first meeting, and of my saying when I saw the photograph of her son Jonathan that it made me 'want to start again,' he said – 'From that moment his goose was cooked.'

And the reality now seemed to be that I wanted my goose to be cooked.

Verity's divorce came through. Rosemary and I initiated proceedings. I did not know how much this might be distressing for Rosemary, but there seemed no other way to go forward. She had a lover in the Isle of

Man, who had a wife and a large family close by with whom he lived. I had met them all on one of my visits, and we had all got on quite well.

When I settled in with Verity I had planned to write an account of what I hoped would be my determined efforts to be a good husband and father. But Verity did not immediately become pregnant, and there were other writing commitments to be finished. I had been diverted from continuing with my 'Play for Not Acting' in order to write the biography of a First-World-War soldier and poet, Julian Grenfell, who had been killed in 1915. He had been Rosemary's uncle, her mother's elder brother; and now all his and other family papers had come down to Rosemary who most generously said I could have the use of them. I had for long been interested in Julian as someone who seemed to have seen the falsity and lunacy of the grandiose Edwardian society around him; he had tried to break away, and had failed. Or rather, the First World War had come along just in time for him to be killed, and thus to become a hero to the society from which he had felt so alien.

The evening before Verity and I were to be married, she remembers, I was so unpleasant to her that she went to Dr Main in the morning and poured this out to him. He took her head in his hands and said 'You don't have to marry him you know.'

But all this seemed to be part of our recognition of challenge. And Verity was a fighter.

Verity and I were married in a registry office with my two elder children as witnesses. They, and Rosemary's and my two younger children who were still at school, knew they had a home in Church Row to which they could always come when they were not in the Isle of Man with Rosemary. Verity had the care of her son Jonathan, and sooner or later we would have a child of our own. So we had the makings of an extended family to which I could one day write about my efforts to be a good father; and in the meantime I could get on with the Julian Grenfell book, working from the mass of papers that were spread out in one of the studios at the bottom of the garden.

So long as I was doing the Grenfell book I could talk about this without difficulty to Fordham, who perhaps saw parallels between Julian's story and my own. But then the time came when the book was done, and I was going back to my play – although I was now thinking that to demonstrate what I wanted perhaps there had to be two or even three plays with the same actors acting different characters in different settings in each. By this means, I imagined, an audience might see how one person might become as it were a different character in different circumstances; although somewhere off-stage there was, or should be, the person who he or she 'really' was. By people becoming aware of this way of seeing things they might also perhaps recognise the 'unreality' of the histrionics in which they and others indulged as it were on stage. I would be trying to say – It's not so much that people can make themselves stop behaving like Othello or Macbeth, as that they might with part of themselves learn to see that, when they are so behaving, they are engaged in no more than a perhaps distressing but basically ephemeral stage-performance.

But in trying to explain this to Fordham I was apt to become once more inarticulate. I would say – But I'm saying that such stuff can hardly be talked about! It can only be demonstrated in the context of a stage.

Fordham would say – But if you can't talk about what's going on in your mind, how can your analysis continue?

I said – Yes I see that.

I wondered – Analysts have to say that it is impossible to analyse oneself?

When Verity and I had been holidaying in the island of Djerba soon after we had met, I had been reading a book by Fordham and we were pleased when I came across a quote from Verity's Dr Main, which said

'The difficulty with self-analysis is in the counter-transference.' When I had worked this out, I found it both witty and slightly disturbing.

Now in my analysis Fordham seemed to be suggesting that unless the style of what was going on in my mind changed, my analysis might have to end.

Well so be it; was not my first loyalty to my plays?

So after time I wrote to Fordham saying I was grateful to him for all the help and insights he had given me, but if it seemed I could not talk intelligibly about what he wanted me to talk about, then perhaps, yes, there was no point in my analysis carrying on.

He wrote to say he thought I was wrong about this, and he would keep the times of my sessions open for a week or two. But it seemed to me that he was still not seeing my predicament, and so I did not go back.

(He had once said to me about my script-writing film jobs – You don't stick with your commitments! You abandon them to go your own way! I had said – You think that is wrong?)

Verity however was anxious about my leaving Fordham. He had provided some safety net to our marriage – in the manner, could it be said, of the old God of the Garden of Eden? And now that the book about Julian Grenfell was finished, would Verity feel the same threat from my plays as Fordham had done?

Wives are renowned for having difficulty with writers appearing to be unfaithful to them with their books – the 'mistresses in their heads.'

And what if these mistresses are things that writers say they find it impossible to talk about!

Verity and I went on a camping holiday in Italy towing a trailer tent behind the car and taking Jonathan, aged three, with us. We stopped at Assisi, and knelt in a row beneath Giotto's fresco of the Flight of the

Holy Family to Egypt, and prayed for a baby. Soon after we got home Verity found she was pregnant.

I wondered – But now, will there not be other demands on a good breast?

But in writing my plays, was I not trying to grow up – to be weaned?

19

I have not known how to write this last part of *Paradoxes of Peace*. I want it to be the story of a good marriage: not one that is uneventful and boring such as Tolstoy said would not be worth writing about, but one in which each partner has a strong desire to learn and to get the best out of what might be possible worlds. This would naturally contain instances akin to the experiences of the prodigal sibling whom his father blessed, as well as those of the stay-at-home brother who was rewarded. There is indeed the matter of one of the cornerstones of this book – that those whom Jesus loved were not those who saw themselves as without sin, but those who saw themselves as sinners like everyone else, and it was by the admission of this that there was made possible the operation of grace.

But it is just one's own sins that one has to admit; not those of other people. Concerning theirs, there is the requirement to forgive. This is (or should be) a keystone of Christian teaching.

But how does one then tell truly the story of a marriage which is between two people? Should one try to tell it from two points of view? But one has no right to think one can tell truly another person's view!

I suggested to Verity that she should write her own account of our marriage, or at least a commentary on where she thought I was getting my account wrong, and these could be slotted into this book. But this proved to be cumbersome, and has not worked out.

But the edict remains that in giving an account of even a roller-coaster marriage one should take note of one's own difficulties and where one has gone wrong, and should leave the experience of another to forgiveness. This is what Christians are told, and what better can one do.

But Jesus also told people whom he had healed to keep the news secret – perhaps because inquisitors would find things to mock and condemn, which is the style of media people today. But it seems to me that it is this fashion that should be challenged.

At the time of my writing, Verity and I have been married some thirty-three years. I am now eighty-four and partly disabled, and Verity looks after me meticulously. She is loved and revered as a wife, mother, stepmother, grandmother and stepgrandmother. She works successfully with patients as a psychotherapist. About the business of healing, self-healing, and of damaged creatures 'coming through,' what more need be said?

*

The first two or three years of Verity's and my marriage were sensuous and orderly; we each needed to be nourished after the difficulties of our recent pasts and childhoods. But then – how does one grow up?

When Freudians or Kleinians talk of a good breast they presumably refer to a style of nurturing without conflict or dissimulation. But in family life, however good, there is always some natural conflict of interests. Not just with rival demands of work and family, but husbands and children for instance are seen to have a hard time if the attention of wives and mothers is turned from one to the other. Verity had made clear her passion to have a new baby. But then could not I, faced with the likely transference of her attention, now use this chance not to resent nor muscle in on Verity's new preoccupation, but to grow up and learn to be a good husband and family man by attending to my work, my plays, as it were to my own babies in my head? But life seldom allows things to be so reasonable. And pregnant mothers more than most people perhaps need the best of both worlds – those of absorption in baby, and attention of husband.

Verity went into her love-affair with her pregnancy. I tried to conjure out of the air my *Plays for Not Acting* – hardly a natural procreation. (Was I hoping – ha ha – for some immaculate conception?)

Before Verity had become pregnant we had for financial reasons let the big house in Church Row and moved at least temporarily into the studio-cottages at the end of the garden. Here, we now planned for Verity to give birth in currently fashionable 'natural' conditions – at home with sweet music playing and a warm bath in which the new-born baby could be immersed to lessen the shock of eviction from the womb. But when the time approached there was said to be a fault in the sugar content of Verity's blood, and the baby could be seen to have a big head. So we were advised that Verity should go into hospital; even that it might be necessary for her to have a caesarean operation. However in the hospital she hung on; and I assured the doctors she would want the birth to be as natural as possible. And before too long the baby emerged with a whoosh. The rugger-playing gynaecologist held up our son Marius by the ankles and said 'He'll make a prop forward!' And might it not be an evolutionary advantage to have a big head?

Then when Verity and Marius arrived home he seemed, as babies do, an overwhelmingly self-obsessed presence. Cast out of Eden, and in the wilderness being totally dependent on the attention of others, how do babies survive except by alarming or charming those around them, to keep them on their toes?

At first I tried to take my turn at sitting by our baby's cot at night while he cried. Then it seemed that I was just part of the context in which he was making his protest against the world at large, and it was the babies in my head that were suffering from a more remediable neglect. So I tip-toed away and cobbled up a bed in an outhouse where we usually kept garden tools. Verity seemed better at sleeping through noise than I. So I took to sleeping regularly in my own would-be silent womb or tomb. But it was I who had turned my attention from Verity, and not her from me. This was the first testing of strain of the (necessary?) paradox between freedom and fidelity.

Then – where was I to work during the day? There was no spare space in the cottages, in which hubbub continued. So I got hold of another garden shed, wooden and ramshackle, and set it up on a piece of flat roof. This I climbed up to by ladder each morning – happily in summer, then in winter I froze. So after a while I looked for and found a basement room a few hundred yards from Church Row which I could rent; and I took to going there each morning with a bundle of papers under my arm.

And on the way I might talk to myself as if on a stage – No I'm not running away; yes of course I'm running away –

– Well what's wrong with running away? Did I say there was anything wrong with running away? –

And so on.

Ah the jolly game of being both actor and audience!

But this was a game that Rosemary and I had found it difficult enough to play, and Rosemary had been conditioned to bargain for this sort of thing more than Verity.

And then when I was in my room which was supposed to be a haven from the on-stage distractions of family life – but which in fact seemed more like a vacuum chamber –

– I would sit-

– and walk around –

– and sit and stare at my typewriter –

– and remember how I had once thought that the best condition in which to write might be that of a prisoner in a cell –

– but this was nothing like a world off-stage –

– it was just like the setting for a drama about a prisoner in a cell.

It began to seem that *Plays for Not Acting* might better be titled *Writing that Cannot Be Written*. I was trying to convey a sense of my characters (and thus readers or audience) being aware of things going on elsewhere ('off-stage') which they felt were happening, must be happening, although they had no means of knowing just what they were. Would not (should not) this be like one's experience of God? If one had anything that could be called a sense of God, would one not have the impression that He was there, and up to something, although one should properly not quite know what this was? Or if one claimed one did, then one would be committing the absurdity of putting oneself in the place of God. But how to work on such ideas in one's own mind, let alone convey them to the minds of others?

Had Fordham been right – that one cannot wait in one's mind for one's mind to become aware of what is not there? One might protect oneself from distractions, but what one hopes might come in from off-stage would be not a matter of manipulation but of grace. Had I not learned this years ago! So what was I doing now banged-up in a cell like a monk or a criminal! Oh yes, one's mind was composed of what were called cells. So what might the mind of a monk or a criminal find coming in?

Emerging from the woodwork of what I must have imagined to be the ivory tower of my mind there would creep – not angels or muses from Parnassus; not even childish yearnings of need or greed, stock invasions of irritation and resentment – but bizarre emanations of forces both more primitive and yet sophisticated – forces which had spun humans out of chaos or slime; seeds of birth containing knowledge of death; delight that embraces pain; dirt that shines with the promise of ease and relaxation –

– refugees from knocking-shop or harem; dusky maidens or Breughelesque bum-boys; satyrs and nymphets; dominatrices and bondsmen. Where do they come from; where are they going? Are they the all-too-visible manifestations of the invisible dark matter that hurls the universe apart as well as holds it together; that tethers humans to earth as if strapped into a roller coaster; that gets us stretching for forbidden fruits not knowing if these might be for salvation or damnation? So if my analyst had been right, and words cannot handle this – then what is the end of this sentence? Is there an end to it? – Hullo Hullo! Let's have a look at you! Fancy your turning up here! Oh yes, I know I did say come up and see me some time. I am, after all, a writer. And writers are easy meat, aren't they? So let's get on with it. That's what they say, isn't it –

'Make you comfy'?

– In massage parlours all over the world: when changing babies' nappies –

And then the blessed release which wipes things out like a tsunami –

– Except possibly the lucky two-by-twos who have gone into an ark.

Good heavens, it's half past five! Soon time to be going home.

But I've got nothing done! Well nothing that can be called anything. But isn't that the sort of thing I'm supposed to be imagining?

My characters are in a theatre. There is a revolution going on outside. Should they pay attention to it? Should they get on with their play?

What else can they do –

– Pay attention to what's going on elsewhere?

Good heavens, it's half past six! Time for a Guinness.

(Who was it who said that? Oh yes, the man in the next bed in the hospital near Bath.)

Pay attention to what matters.

I can say – Sorry I'm so late, but just as I'm leaving to come home there's always just one more thing coming into my head. So I have to write it down.

– In the pub?

– Yes. Well just for a minute.

Next time perhaps I'll say I had to go to the public library.

I like this pub. You can feel you are off-stage. You can sit and watch, and people get on with their performances.

– What sort of things do you have to write down?

– Oh, just that we're all trapped in the small circle of our heads, from which we never see out. It was this that made Kleist despair –

– Oh Kleist! You're always on about Kleist! He killed himself didn't he?

– Yes.

– I hate it when you go on about things like that.

– He said we had to go right round the world and get at the tree of knowledge again by the back way.

– Well perhaps you can do it a bit quicker next time.

This is in my mind. But now, approaching my home – Why can't I see my home as my infinity off-stage? Our studio-cottages with their lovely garden of roses, ceramic fountain, winter-flowering cherry; iconic wife and child –

'Hullo.'

'Hullo.'

'I was expecting you at half past five.'

'There's always just one more thing to write down.'

'Such as – '

'Oh I'm trying to write these plays, you know, about how can we get out of the confines of our minds.'

'And can you?'

'One can try.'

Verity would have been waiting in the studio which was her stage-set with her baby, her three year son that earlier she would have picked up from school, the cat, toys on the floor, a packet of Wheatabix on the table, a contraption hung by elastic from the ceiling in which the baby could one day bounce itself up and down. Verity would have seen me approaching up the hill an alien from another world –

I say – 'I'm sorry.'

'I do hate it when – '

'When what – '

'No I don't mean that!'

So you learn to wait, and watch, do you? And then things either work themselves out or they do not.

At the time of my writing this, as I have said, Verity and I have been married for some thirty-three years. We have loved each other, laughed a lot with each other, cursed each other, hurled things at each other. We have walked out declaiming in tragic-heroic style that we never want to see each other again; then have returned and cannot quite remember how we imagined we might do without each other. We have had times so happy and fruitful that our Garden has seemed like an orchard of nothing-forbidden trees. Then we have had the fun-fair terrors of a roller coaster or wall of death. We have almost never thought we should not be married.

In marriage, in the words of the prayer book, two people become one flesh. There are thus so many chances for each to get under the skin of the other that one becomes – all right – either a monster or an art-work. Or both. Well why not? This may be the style – not other than God; not other than evolution – of escape from being trapped in one's own head.

Two by two into an ark? A lifetime's work. So better get on with it.

20

While Verity was pregnant with Marius we had been out to Majorca to look at a bit of land by the sea which I had bought in partnership with my brother Michael some years ago when I had been married to Rose- mary. Michael and I had each wanted to get hold of a piece of Medi- terranean coastline before prices became prohibitive, but we neither of us had at the time enough capital to do this on our own, so we had planned to pool our resources. We could think what to do about build- ing on the land later.

We went exploring along the unspoilt south-east coast of Majorca. We found what seemed a perfect piece of land at the back and along a side of one of the island's narrow inlets known as a *calas*, a mile or two from the village of Cala D'Or. We bargained for this land sitting in cafés with the local villagers. This was a complex business because, according to Majorcan law, on the death of a landowner the land and amenities had to be shared between the heirs. Thus the property we were keen on – even the well – was now split between what seemed to be innumer- able interested parties. But eventually we got agreement – and became owners of a sizeable chunk of land around the beautiful *Cala Senau*.

Then things stalled. My brother had brought into partnership a bank- ing friend who could arrange to get money out to Majorca (these were the days of strict exchange-control); but we found it impossible to agree about the sort of house which we all would like to take a turn to holiday in. But then the local council by-passed our problem by designating this whole stretch of coast a green belt area, so it became impossible to build anyway.

My brother and his friend then lost interest. Rosemary and I with our young family went out for two or three summers to camp on the wonderfully empty land. We enjoyed this greatly. Then Rosemary moved to the wilds of the Isle of Man.

I loved this Majorcan land, and it was another story-book Garden of Eden. It was to keep an eye on it that I rented the holiday house with the large flat roof in Cala D'Or. But it seemed that Senau (which means 'his boat') was drifting away from me, because I did not see what use I could make of it on my own.

Then when Verity was expecting Marius, and already had Jonathan now aged three, it seemed that we could soon well do with a holiday home, because in Hampstead we were either on top of each other in the studios or stressfully spread out with bits and pieces let. So I took Verity out to see *Cala Senau*; and as we came round a bend of the bumpy track that my brother and I had made passable there it was – glittering with blue and silver sea and sand. I could see Verity falling in love with the place.

We still could not build, so Verity and I bought cheaply a ruined farmhouse two or three miles inland and made this habitable; and the next summer we moved in, and went down to Senau to picnic and swim each day. We were now grateful that it had been designated a green belt area, because at first there was seldom anyone else there; and then later, as tourism grew, there were just a boatload or two and a few cars that came down the track in the middle of the day and left before evening,

There was a ruined boathouse on our land, which we surreptitiously put a roof and a door on; this we could use as a base for camping and a store. Somewhat later we found an official-looking notice pinned on the door which we feared would be an order to remove the door and the roof; but it was only a demand note for minuscule taxes.

The sandy beach and boathouse and rocky bay – and the farmhouse in the hills which even before we arrived was called *Can Rave* (as if presaging Ravensdale) – became for more than twenty years the magical domain of Verity's and my and our family's happy life. At *Can Rave* we had no telephone and at first no electricity nor piped water; we wound up buckets from a well which collected rainwater; we got a hand pump going, which piped water up to the house for a bath. The used bath water could then be hosed out of the window to irrigate the garden along channels scraped in the earth. Out of the farmyard I made a flower-garden with paths and rough-stone walls; beds of oleander and hibiscus, and a datura with huge white flowers like lilies hanging down. At Senau we swam and lay on the beach and clambered over cliff-like rocks from which, from a great height, one could jump back into the sea. We came across a mysterious hole on our rocky headland down which we could perilously clamber to an otherwise inaccessible bay. Here there were caves and grottos, and an alarming underwater tunnel.

Can Rave and *Cala Senau* became our make-believe Eden. Here Marius learned to walk, Jonathan to swim, both later boldly to climb down the hole in the rocks and explore the secrets of the could-be frightening bay. Jonathan's and Marius's friends came to stay year after year; my older children came together with, soon, my grandchildren. Verity cooked luxuriant meals for large numbers: we ate out of doors at a long table either in the shade of an old implement shed, or at night under the stars. In the garden I grew artichokes and broad beans which, if planted at Christmas, after protective weeds had been cleared, could be picked and eaten at Easter. Towards the end of the summer holidays there were figs and almonds to be gathered; the almonds to be delicately roasted in olive oil.

Verity's and my siblings and friends came to stay. We devised games which were enjoyed by grown-ups and children alike – the catching-on-sight and rescuing game called Lions that I had played as a child and then with such success with my platoon in the war: a game like fives or real tennis in which a ball was hit by hand onto the house's sloping roof and then chased if necessary into the bamboos or cactuses. In the evenings there might be Liar Poker or Scrabble; or just gazing at a log fire or allusively empty grate. Our children's friends became Verity's and my friends. One lost a sense that such happiness might not be permanent.

I have called my story 'Paradoxes of Peace.' But it seemed to me that at *Cala Senau* and *Can Rave* paradoxes, like parallel lines, became one in some sort of infinity. Beneath a golden sky, between the stillness of the hills behind and the vastness of the sea in front, there was just wonder. Humans might learn to remember this.

21

I had sometimes wondered on my dawdling journeys to and from the vacuum-chamber of the room in Hampstead where I tried to write, if I might one day bump into Natalie; but the flat that I had handed over to her was on the other side of London. There were moments when my regression to infantilism returned and I regretted handing over this flat: why should I be generous to her when she had not been generous to me? Blah blah blah. But this throw-back fairly quickly ceased; so might there now be some healing not only in the mind but in the air – how might one imagine it – as the hidden matter which held the universe together? And so might not some bonds which had once been shackles remain as connections by which things could sort themselves out; and what had been suffered as tragedy or farce might be seen as – the stuff of life?

I had the vision, that is, of a sort of cosmic good breast; one that might be available to anyone who might risk not being trapped in the confines of his or her own head. But what would this signify in relation to myself and Natalie: that I would just like to know how she was? I would like her to know that I wished her good rather than ill? But would this show disloyalty to Verity? Or should a cosmic good breast be able to sort out and sustain everyone.

I had for long thought that a personal 'good breast' would be something from which one would have to be weaned: that a good grown-up style of life would surely include risks, ups and downs; the paradox of fidelity and endeavour. And then one day when I was wandering along thinking – Ah angels, devils, breasts; they are just words for what either happens or does not – there she was, Natalie, coming from the direction of Hampstead Heath with a large black dog on a lead; also a man in tow. A new lover? Well what the hell! Though I'd better not look at him too closely. I said 'Oh hullo.' She said 'Hullo.' I said 'Is that your dog?' She said 'Yes.' I thought – Well I might be able to keep an eye out for the dog. But what was she doing up here? It was as if I were seeing her through the wrong end of a telescope. I thought – So that's all right then.

I said 'Well, see you!' We went on. I thought – Didn't Faust see Mephistopheles in the guise of a black dog, sniffing out the way to – damnation? salvation?

Then when I arrived home I wondered – But should I tell Verity? Either way, will I have something to be guilty about?

Time passed. I heard that Natalie had sold the flat which I had given her and bought one in Belsize Park, which was close to Hampstead. Well, she had always liked this part of London. And things would be easier for her, wouldn't they, if she had a lover? Yes, this was better.

I came to the end of my *Plays for Not Acting* – which were now, yes, three short plays combined with four Essays as interludes and a short concluding novel *Cypher*. In the latter the six persons who had acted all the different characters in the different plays came together – yes you've got it! – supposedly off-stage. (My dictionary definition of 'cypher,' which I quoted, was – 'a manner of writing intelligible to those possessing the key . . . also the key to such a system.') And the whole package was entitled *Catastrophe Practice* – a reference to the recently fashionable 'catastrophe theory,' which conjectured that evolution sometimes takes place in sudden jumps in response to catastrophe, in distinction from the orthodox neo-Darwinian view which held that mutations occurred almost infinitesimally.

When the time came for me to go through the script for the last time to pull it together – for it to be ready to be launched like a kite with a long and luminous tail – I wanted more than ever to be free from distractions, so I went with my script to Spain, to a hotel in the hills near Segovia that had once been a monastery. From there I wrote to Verity to say that I wanted to dedicate the work to her with two inscriptions from Nietzsche: the first – 'Supposing truth to be a woman, what? Is the suspicion not well founded that philosophers, when they have been dogmatists, have had little understanding of women?' And the second – 'What meaning would our whole being possess if it were not this – that in us the will to truth becomes conscious of itself as a problem.' I said that this was how I saw Verity and me.

Then I wrote to Rosemary to say that I thought *Catastrophe Practice* was the best thing I had done or ever would do; and I wanted to thank her for all the years of our marriage during which I had been so impossible and she had been so loyal; and this was what had made my writing possible. And then when I got home, I had copies made of *Catastrophe Practice* and parcelled them into fat boxes and sent them off to agent and publisher and the very few friends who I thought might see what I was up to. But then it appeared that no one did.

I told myself – But this is what I've been saying, isn't it? Some outlandish mutation either takes off, or it crashes –

– but some black box might survive among the wreckage?

I would at times vary my now somewhat disheartened walks over Hampstead Heath by going to Primrose Hill. One afternoon there was a large black dog going round and round as if looking for some quarry to flush out. I thought – Well, it could be Mephistopheles. I followed the dog; and there lying on her back on the grass was Natalie. She had her eyes closed but did not seem to be sleeping. I wondered if my observing her would make her wake. She opened her eyes and said 'I was just thinking of you!' I said 'I saw your dog.' She had her hand on the dog which was gazing up at me as if trying to decide whether or not to trust me. I said 'How are the children?' She said 'They're well.' I said 'It would be nice if we could see each other and talk some time.' She said 'Yes that's what I was thinking.'

I thought – It was Goethe who had the idea that Mephistopheles was the force which might enact evil but could engender good.

When I had been living with Natalie I had become friends with Tom Rosenthal, a friend of hers and her husband's (it was he who had told me of her move to Belsize Park). Tom was now managing director of the publishers Martin Secker & Warburg. He had heard about *Catastrophe Practice* and the difficulties it was having with publishers, and he now asked me if he could see the script. So I sent it to him, and after a time by way of response he invited me and Verity to the theatre with himself and his wife Ann. During the first interval (I do not remember the play; I suppose I was preoccupied) Tom said that although he did not pretend fully to understand *Catastrophe Practice*, he recognised good writing when he saw it; and so would publish it, yes; but on condition that I would undertake here and now to write a book about my father which he would publish in due course. I said that I would do this; but it could not be before my father's death. During the second act of the play I calculated that although my father was now in his eighties, I might be able to complete before he died two or three of the novel-sequels to *Catastrophe Practice* that I had been contemplating; and it would surely be in Tom's interests to publish these, once he had published the first book, while he was waiting for the book about my father. So before we left the theatre Tom and I settled our deal. And I thought – What on earth does it matter if no one sees precisely what *Catastrophe Practice* is up to, if there are these extraordinary coincidences and developments going on off-stage.

When publication time came Verity and I invited people to a party for 'catastrophe practice' as if this might be for an activity rather than a book. It was a cold night and we had braziers in the garden. People danced and kept warm; and sometimes leafed through the pages of my book gingerly in the light of the flames. It was a good party; and indeed what did it matter if people did not get the code.

Over the next few years I managed to finish, and Tom to publish, two not-so-outlandish follow-up novels – *Imago Bird* and *Serpent* – about the young man and then the middle-aged couple who could be imagined as having acted three of the parts in the plays. These were persons each wondering how they might stand back from themselves and watch themselves – and thus might avoid being prey to the tendencies nudging much of humanity towards catastrophe.

And as mutations they might be agents in evolution?

This was my fancy.

But what was my own success or failure at dealing with paradoxes at this time?

- 22 -

Verity and I and the children continued to go out to *Can Rave* and *Cala Senau* at Easter and in the summer, and at Christmas as often as this was possible. We towed our trailer tent and set it up in the trees behind the beach at Senau. We took with us our *au pair* Vivien, who became a great friend of ours and of the children. One day a man came wandering down the drive and asked us if we'd like piped water. We said – Yes: when? He said – Tomorrow. They were already making good progress from the village a mile away. And later we got hooked up to mains electricity.

All this meant that we could now build a swimming-pool, and could reasonably and profitably rent out the house when we were not there. So we put the letting in the hands of a local agent, and did not have to worry so much about expense and maintenance. But perhaps some of the magic of the place began to be diluted.

In London I had taken to going down the hill in the afternoons to the public library in Swiss Cottage because I needed to do research for my novel *Serpent*. From the library on my way home I would sometimes call in on Natalie in Belsize Park, and we would talk. There had come about a change, indeed, in how we interacted with one another – all obsession spent, yes, but still a need, as I had felt, for old wounds to be healed and for us to learn not to be destructive towards one another. I had felt that one could not truly be at peace in the present without setting out to lay to rest ghosts of the past. This was part of my image of a cosmic good breast. But was it true? And was it being destructive of my relationship with Verity? I had still not told Verity that I had again come across Natalie.

Even before this, Verity had begun to show distress and anger at my absences owing to my obsession with my work; and I had found myself becoming angry back. When I could, I would turn and run from anger – especially now when I was aware that Verity's anger could be justified since I was not telling her that I was occasionally seeing Natalie. But then Verity would write me notes apologising for her anger –

But did this increase my guilt rather than absolve it?

I could not work out what was the proper thing to do. Should fidelity to one's marriage preclude things that seemed kind and sensible outside it?

Probably, yes.

But soon there were other ghosts coming roaring out of the past.

I was just embarking on the fourth book of my *Catastrophe Practice* series, a novel to be called *Judith* – the young girl of my six characters in search of a mutation – when my father died. I was glad that I had my arrangement with Tom Rosenthal, but I was not at all sure what I would be able to write about my father; would I be able to get hold of papers necessary to write anything more than a personal memoir, leaving others to write what they would of his public life from his own and public archives? During his last years I had got on well with my father; we had re-established something of our old war-time intimacy when he had been in jail and I had gone to fight in Italy. In old age he had for some time been out of politics; he had Parkinson's disease. Verity and I would go and stay with him and Diana at their house at Orsay, outside Paris; and he and I would talk. He and Verity got on well together; they would flirt decorously in the manner of disparate people each giving an outing to a common expertise. With Diana's sometimes unguarded opinions Verity found herself with more of a problem. Diana and I however could slip back into the sort of relationship we had had when I was a schoolboy and could question her about her liking for Hitler; and she could sometimes laugh at my jokes.

The last time Verity and I had been to Orsay was, as it happened, a week or so before my father died. He would emerge from his bedroom mid-morning and produce a bottle of pink champagne; he wanted to talk with me about the past – about the time when he had been married to my mother; about what had gone wrong and what might have gone right. It was then that he said – Do you think if I had spent less time in pursuit of women I might have done better in politics? And I said – Dad, you might have done much worse! And he laughed.

He told me the story of how, after my mother's death, he had carried on love-affairs throughout the thirties with both Diana and my mother's younger sister Baba – about most of which I knew, because they had made no effort to conceal it. But now he told me that after the war Baba had come to him and suggested that this arrangement should start up again and continue as before – she had after all, she said, been instrumental, through her friendship with the former Foreign Secretary Lord Halifax, in helping to get my father and Diana out of jail and into house arrest in 1943. My father told me he had felt obliged to say No to Baba's suggestion: his loyalty must be now to Diana, who had spent three and a half years in jail with him. But ever since, Baba had acted hurt and angry towards him like a woman scorned. He ended this story by saying – Do you think I did right? I said – Dad, it must be one of the most right things you've ever done!

I began to have a vision of how I might write about him even in politics as being a sort of pantomime villain – a Mephistopheles whose job it was, as in *Faust*, to challenge and provoke. (When he had been in prison this was sometimes how he had seemed to see himself.) For some time recently I had been murmuring to him that one day some- one should write a book about him (I had not told him of my deal with Tom) that would look at more than the disastrous manifestations of his politics – look at his idealism and love of life as well as his dubious morality. He had not been responding to this; and I was still in the dark about what would eventually be available to me from which I could write. Then at lunch that day – the last Sunday that I saw him – he grew pensive for a while; and then announced formally in front of Diana and Verity that when he died he wished me to have all his papers.

This seemed to me to be both miraculous, and the result of our old war-time intimacy. He knew how much I disapproved of, and indeed had railed against, most of his politics; but even this might have formed part of his trust now that I would always try to tell the truth.

But I still did not know how much Diana, who would have control of the papers, would honour what he had said.

After his death, I thought it would not be good tactics to pursue the matter too quickly; also I was trying to reach some suitable pausing- place in *Judith*. But then I had a letter from Diana reminding me of my father's request, and saying that on account of there being so little storage space in their small house at Orsay, after their house in Ireland had been damaged by fire in the 1950s all of my father's papers that could be rescued had gone for safe keeping to Lismore Castle, the Irish home (though seldom lived in) of her sister and brother-in-law, Debo and Andrew Devonshire. She, Diana, was going to Lismore very shortly when Debo and Andrew would be there; and if I came too I could see what papers I needed. She did not know herself what papers my father had kept: much of the old political archive had been taken away by the security people in 1940. So I put *Judith,* my current example of catastrophe practice, on hold, and flew to Ireland.

When I reached Lismore I found footmen carrying huge bundles of letters up from the cellars and dumping them on the table in the billiards room. I still did not know what I would find: what had my father felt worth preserving? Then out of this seemingly bottomless bran-tub there appeared – good Lord! – letters to and from my mother in her childhood; letters to and from her friends during her brief later life. Then letters and documents from or about me and my sister in our childhood, school reports, letters from our nanny to my mother (including the correspondence about my gin-soaked wet-nurse). How on earth had all this survived? I formed my own huge bundle to carry home.

In London Verity and I had moved back into the big house in Church Row and now the studios were let. But Verity had been having such difficulty with my continuing obsession about my work – and the holidays in *Can Rave* and *Cala Senau* now seemed not so much of a help – that I did not want to bring all my father's papers to Church Row and there spread out the evidence of my mother's and father's disastrous marriage. So I took another solitary room down the hill near the Swiss Cottage library – though Natalie as it happened had by this time returned to her native America, apparently with the prospect of a new marriage.

So within this would-be protected space again I laid out the glimpses of my mother's and father's marriage – and of my and my sister's supposedly traumatic childhood. I became besieged, almost engulfed, by all this; papers took over the table and chairs and even the bed. The room had a basin and a gas-ring, so I could spend days and nights there if I liked. The letters told the story of my father's philandering, yes; of my mother's inability to react to this other than by nagging and complaint, about which she afterwards felt remorse. My father had thus been given chances to run off when he wished, and then to return with honeyed words. And so it went on. This pattern emerged at first largely from letters to my mother from her sisters and friends, who would say – Why don't you go off and have an affair of your own? But it could be inferred from their frustration that she replied that she could not bear to. There were almost no intimate letters that must have existed between my father and my mother. I thought my father must have burnt them.

But then I became aware – was not this pattern of complaint and resentment one that was emerging between Verity and me? She continued to be distressed and angry at my absences, and then I would feel I had an excuse to go off again. Then she would write me notes of apology; but I still was not clear what the effect of these should be. Surely in relevant ways I was so unlike my father! Was not obsession with my work justifiable? Such a corny predicament! So was I not the one who had cause to be aggrieved? My mother had had the means to go off on her own: would not this have been better than to enable people to say she had died of a broken heart? Verity had said – But people do die of a broken heart! I said – And leave two small children?

But was I now suggesting that Verity should have a separate life of her own – as Rosemary had done? Well, perhaps we then at least might learn something that had never been learnt between my father and my mother.

I did in fact make a new friend at this time, a young married woman who had briefly known my father. She was as enthusiastic and helpful about my writing about him as Verity was antagonistic. This friend would come and visit me in my bed-sitting room in Swiss Cottage, and by her encouragement I was heartened to press on with my alarming book, which I foresaw rightly would provoke much all-round family hostility. I made no secret of my new friendship. But would it have been better if I had done?

Then Diana asked me to come and stay at Orsay because she had so much more to tell me. So I went, and was put up in my father's old room, and it was now Diana who was waiting in the mornings ready to talk. At first we kept off politics. She seemed eager to tell me what she knew of my father's infidelities – with whom, when and where, how many times. I wrote these details down in my notebook. But they were all to do with the time of my father's marriage to my mother; and I worked out later that of course Diana must have been telling me all this in order to absolve herself from some of the blame for my mother's much-talked-about broken heart. I did not ask Diana what she thought of my father's very public affair with the young aristocratic girl in the 1950s when he was married to her, Diana, although I knew that she had known about this.

Then she handed me a packet of letters that she said my father always kept under his pillow. She said she had just glanced at them, and they were very sad, but she thought I should have them. They were the intimate letters over the years between my mother and father. I sat up at night reading them.

There was, yes, the almost endlessly repeated pattern – suspicion or evidence of infidelity, my mother's nagging, my father's denials dissolving into rage. Then his storming out of the house taking the chance doubtless to pursue more infidelity; and my mother trying to pursue him with notes of apology that were at times almost abject in their efforts to get him back. I thought with alarm – Indeed there is an echo of this – but only an echo! – between me and Verity. And then my father, on his way home, would be writing my mother cajoling, adoring notes in baby-talk language saying surely she must know that she was the only person he could ever love; that whatever other signs there might be were just silliness. And he would embellish these notes with little drawings of the baby-names he had for my mother – his mutton, his turtle, his piglet. And I thought – So that thus they might remain as children forever?

Then – Well for God's sake, at least Verity and I will not end up like this!

Also in my father's old bedroom where I sat up at nights reading what seemed to be not-after-all forbidden secrets, was a cupboard now stacked with letters to Diana that she must have thought worth preserving from the 1930s. Some of these were from Germany – from Hitler's adjutant, from Goebbels's wife Magda, dozens from Diana's sister Unity. Diana had not told me that I should not look at these, so I had more sleepless nights sitting up deciphering them and making notes of one or two – I did not think I should ask to take any home. One passage that I copied out in order to make sure of remembering it was in a letter from Unity when she had been in Hitler's entourage staying at Obersalzberg. The punch-line of this was – 'I can't tell you how wonderful the Fuhrer was today copying a woman buying a hat! We all nearly died of laughing!'

I thought – Well, talk of *commedia*!

Talk of the games of children.

When I got back from this trip to Orsay I found Verity more than ever distressed that in writing about my father I might be trying to excuse his infidelities and thus what might be my own. My excuse for my absences was that I was finding it increasingly difficult to know how to write about my father and mother, and I needed (selfishly, yes) to be able to try to concentrate free from distraction. I foresaw the hostility that I would be facing from almost all members of my family – it would be felt that I was betraying either my father or my mother or both – and I could not bear it if Verity was now feeling that I was in some way betraying her. I had either to give up, or to fight to keep going.

My father's attitude to marriage was typical of his class and generation. He looked on sexual infidelity as 'doing what came naturally': he had no regard for what might be felt as any supernatural injunction. I had for a time been respectful to conventional Christian injunctions; then I had been struck by the paradoxes concerning sin and infidelity that both Jesus and St Paul had remarked on and had come up with their enigmatic attitudes. It was wrong to be unfaithful, yes: yet 'doing what came naturally' might produce open-heartedness and thus a state of grace. To be sure, such paradoxes were different from my father's simple attitudes; but they too could all too easily lead to deception and self-deception.

There was the further question about the obligation to be truthful. Jesus had often simply parried questions seemed designed to catch him out. It seemed that my father had begun by trying to be honest with my mother; then when this caused pain he had stopped. But in ceasing to be honest, pain had not stopped. And there the two of them seemed to be stuck. But now was I hoping that with Verity there might be a way in which pain and resentment would stop; or that, more in the nature of things, one might learn to put up with them?

Both my mother and Verity seemed to feel, as my heroine in *Impossible Object* had felt, that love, marriage, fidelity, should be all-of-a-piece and faultless: and when it was not, what was there to do but complain? After a time Verity came to see that my mother's cycle of complaint and rage and apology was useless; but she had not at first complied with the idea that my mother should have gone off and played my father at his own game – if not to have affairs, then just to have a life of interests and friendships of her own. (There is evidence that my father would have felt challenged and reined in by this.) However as time went on Verity did indeed get away to enjoy other relationships on her own; but this belongs to a slightly later part of the story.

There came a time when I had come to the end of what I saw as a first volume about my father. I had worked obsessively, and had found so much material that I thought I should make a break in the book after my mother's death, and my publishers Secker & Warburg agreed. (Tom Rosenthal had moved on to manage Andre Deutsch). That is – the death-scene of my mother made such a dramatic and tragic climax that Secker thought they should publish straight away a first volume up to this point, and leave the bulk of my father's fascist years till later. I was quite pleased with this plan because it would give me a breathing space; and I sent off a copy of the script of this first volume to Diana for her approval. I enclosed a note saying that I expected there would be some bits she would not wholly like, but I hoped she would feel I had tried to be truthful.

I got a kind and moving letter back saying my script was 'fascinating, beautifully written, excellent, funny.' She wanted to assure me that she had only glanced at the packet of my mother's letters she had handed to me, so she had not realised how much my mother minded my father's infidelity. If she had done at the time, she said, perhaps she might have behaved differently. I replied that I was most grateful for her generous letter, because it was important to me that my book should seem fair to all concerned.

Then a week or two later Diana wrote that she had had a change of mind and heart; she now saw the book as a bitter attack on my father and all he stood for, and one which only a treacherous member of his family could have written. She said she would do everything to stop the second volume being published, which in theory she could do, because she owned so many of the copyrights. I asked my alarmed publishers please to pay little attention to these threats because I was confident they would not be carried out. I had become accustomed to Diana's violent and virulent swings of mood at the time when she had first called me an angel for helping Alexander to escape from the influence of his father; then had berated me for not being more of an authoritarian figure myself. I explained to Secker that Diana had passionate loyalty to my father, but at the same time a rare ability to recognise what aimed at being true. Which of these two attributes came out on top usually depended on what was practical. So if they, my publishers, got fulminating letters from Diana's lawyers, could they please ask, as lawyer's do, for elucidation point by point – and carry on both with the publication of this volume and preparations for the second. This they most trustingly did: and by the time the second volume was ready for the printers Diana had in fact withdrawn all her objections – even those about the inclusion of her own letters to my father. But she said she would never speak to me again; and she never did.

I came to think that Diana's change of heart to hostility about the first volume was probably due not so much to the exposure of my father's painful relationship with my mother, as to my treatment of his politics as being at heart not serious. My contention was that he had seen and enjoyed himself as a magnificent one-man-band; but for instance he had not worked laboriously to bring any member of his party close to being in a position of power – even in local government. Diana was capable of glimpsing and accepting where both he and she had gone wrong in a tragic and grandiose manner: she had in fact in a rare moment of vulnerability after his death said to me – 'I think the day that I met Hitler was the day that ruined my life'; and had added – 'And your father's.' However, what seemed unbearable for her to admit was that my father's career as a fascist when he had been in close relationship with her, had been for the most part blinkered folly.

A more urgent cause of trauma for me occurred when I showed the script of the first volume to Verity. She was then able to read the intensely sad letters that my mother had written to my father, and indeed felt more that ever that she could see patterns that had begun to form between herself and me. She said she did not think the book should be published in its present form; that my publishers were rushing it into print heedlessly hoping to cash in on the dramatic sadness of my mother's death. Recently when Verity had been enraged with me she would cry – 'Your father killed your mother and now you will kill me!' I resented this: I thought I was having enough battles with Diana and my siblings. This was a time when Verity and I were living very much apart: I was either in my Swiss Cottage room, or in one of the cottages at the bottom of the garden, while she and the children were in the Church Row house. And my feelings were becoming increasingly stressed and confused – as indeed is my ability nowadays to remember precise details of this time.

My publishers planned to give an evening publication party for the first volume to which, Verity remembers, she was not invited, and I remember that she said she would not come. My friend who had been encouraging me with the book said she would have people in to an early supper before going on to the party; I said I would attend this. Verity, naturally, minded this; it seemed that our marriage was reaching a pitch at which it might break.

The time before the publisher's party, and indeed the party itself, were fraught. Might in fact Verity's and my marriage be ending in tragedy like that of my father and mother? There was one way in which I had sometimes behaved worse to Verity than my father ever had to my mother, which was that when we were both in extreme distress I had sometimes lashed out and hit her. This is a sin that is humanly inexcusable, yes. But there is some (inexcusable) instinct that it may be a way to bring at least to a temporary end what seems to be an endless cycle of bitterness and recrimination, just because of the obvious horror of what has occurred and because the recipient of the violence can feel she has proved her point – See what a cruel brute you are! On the other hand might not Verity now justifiably feel that our marriage should be over? Anyway, after the traumas of the publishing party, which Verity indeed did not attend, I did not think that she and I should confront one another just yet. We needed a break for each to stand back from the other. And circumstances had become such that Verity seemed to agree.

In the course of writing about my father and my mother I had begun to feel – but was becoming increasingly less clear-headed or clear-hearted – that if there was anyone towards whom it could be said that I had behaved badly in the way that my father had behaved towards my mother, then surely it was my first wife Rosemary. But Rosemary had retreated into herself and her work, and had tried to carry on, as I had, with a sort of life that she had wanted – until, that is, Verity had turned up and had wanted fidelity in marriage, and by this time I had felt that this was what I wanted too. But then was it not Rosemary who had been abandoned – although she had still managed to get on with her life, going on long trips with her paints to Australia, New Mexico, California. She had spent winters in these places; and had created something of the life she had wanted. But she had thus to a large extent separated herself from her children; and was I not largely responsible for this, having rendered life sad and difficult at home?

And now, concurrently with the publication of my first volume about my father and its attendant dramas, I had been hearing – not from Rosemary herself but through the children – that she was ill in California, and was confined to bed, and was making no effort to get home. And her children, our children, were concerned about this. Rosemary now had grandchildren she had never seen.

So it struck me that what I should do now, in this situation of multiple trauma and stand-off, was to check that Verity was what could be called all right, but not to hurry to her with the inevitability of recrimination or apology by which the cycle of anger and guilt and pain might go on for ever; even, as with my mother, end in death? So I sent a message to Verity to say that since we were getting on so badly, I was taking the opportunity to fly out to California and visit Rosemary, who it appeared was ill and would not or could not get out of bed. I might be able to persuade her to come home for proper treatment. In any case, it would give me something useful (I trusted) to do, while the recriminations settled down about my book. And I hoped to goodness that Verity would see it like this, because she surely wouldn't want me hanging around just now or just yet. (I did not, I trust, embark on my blather about all this fulfilling the requirements of an as-it-were global good breast.)

So I flew to California. The story that I had heard from my children was that Rosemary had gone into hospital to have a small non-malignant growth removed from her inside; and there, while under anaesthetic, some accident had occurred which had left her with an injury to her back. A doctor who had become her friend had confessed that it was likely that when she was being carried on a stretcher the hospital porters, high on dope, might have dropped her. If she sued the hospital she might get damages of hundreds of thousands of dollars; but for two or three years she would have to appear and behave exactly as her lawyer told her – in the manner, that is, of a distraught and ruined victim. To Rosemary this had seemed absurd. So with the help of friends she had rented an apartment near the sea-front in Santa Monica and there, waited on daily by a Filipino maid, she propped herself up in bed and continued to paint or draw, and to entertain friends who came to visit her. This seemed to me an admirable making the best of a grievous situation. But our children felt, and I agreed, that Rosemary would be more likely to get well if she came home.

I had divorced Rosemary in order to marry Verity. But in what I imagined as the world off-stage I had never felt totally severed from Rosemary. Once people have married, that is, are they not in the position of those particles which, once they have been joined, are in some infinity always connected even if at opposite ends of the universe? (I have said this before? But this is such a part of what I mean by things going on off stage!)

I had managed to telephone Rosemary from Heathrow, and she seemed to be glad that I was coming. From Los Angeles airport I checked in late in the evening at a small hotel in Santa Monica. There, totally unexpectedly, I found my old friend Timmy from my schooldays and the war; he had once been in love with Rosemary, and then had become an actor and had married and become a priest. I had not seen him for some years. It appeared that he too had heard Rosemary was ill and had, like me, come to visit her and to see if there was anything he could do. I was extraordinarily glad to see him. It was by now too late at night for me to go on to Rosemary, and Timmy said that he was booked to fly back to London in the morning having been in Santa Monica for three days. So in the hotel we sat up and drank whisky and chewed over old times, and what was happening in the present. It seemed to me that meeting Timmy and once more getting on so well, was a portent that other things might work out in as good a way as I had dared hope.

If things are risked, that is, do they not sometimes work out in ways that indeed one had hardly dared hope? This had been my experience in war. But as well as the readiness to risk, there is also the folklore (touch wood!) not to talk about it too much. So all right, everything is just chance, yes.

The next morning Rosemary was propped up in bed, looking well. We were shy but not too shy with one another; it was as if this odd meeting were after all natural and proper. She told me the story of her injured back without resentment or self-pity; she said she was happy to be where she was, with loyal and interesting friends. And she had a nice doctor who was, yes, perhaps a bit in love with her. And her loyal Filipino maid. And she could look out of the window and watch the comings and goings of humanity on the Santa Monica promenade, including the devotees of the latest mystical cult doing their strange exercises of pushing against trees. And she could sketch them. Also she was in a group with an analyst who was a powerful Hollywood guru: it was he, yes, who was advising her not to go back to England. He said that her children were now old enough not to need her; and had she not been having sad times with her old family anyway. But she said she would appreciate it, yes, if I would see this guru and talk to him. And she was glad that I had come.

I spent a week in Santa Monica. When I was not with Rosemary I visited the museums and galleries of Los Angeles; I drove up the hill to look at the observatory with the enormous telescope that was exploring particles in outer space. When I was with Rosemary we carried on in the style in which we had been at ease in the early days of our marriage; we had often indulged in a sort of playful make-believe.

Three occasions stay in my mind of our time in Santa Monica. The first was when Rosemary invited to a party some of her new friends so that I could meet them. I said I would be responsible for drinks and snacks. Rosemary hardly bothered to introduce me; she seemed to assume that her friends would know who I was. They were painters, writers, musicians. They of course knew that Rosemary and I were no longer married; but it seemed not improper to imagine that we might be.

The second instance was when she was restless one morning and she said she needed to get someone in to massage her feet. I said that I would do this. She said 'Do you know how?' I said 'There can't be many options.' So she lay back on her bed and I squeezed and kneaded her feet, and she never stopped talking. I said 'You're supposed to relax.' She said 'I know.' I said 'In the old days, it was me who couldn't stop talking.'

The third instance was when she asked her analyst to come round and meet me. This he did one evening after he had been playing tennis.

He was an imposing, stylish man with white hair and wearing white shorts. Rosemary said 'Nick would like to talk to you.' He said 'What about?' I said 'I think Rosemary should come home; there doesn't seem to be any reason for her to get well here.' He said to Rosemary 'And what do you think about that?' She said 'I don't know.' He said to me 'Her divorce was a great shock to her; she has become better here.' I said 'Yes, but now you seem to be keeping her here.' He had a glass of wine, and then left. A day or two later I flew home. Not long after, one of our sons went out and helped her pack and escorted her home. In London, she had an operation on her back that was at least temporarily successful.

I had thought that when I got home I might find myself and Verity still in a ghastly sitcom-style drama in which people have endlessly re-peated confrontations because that is what they have been programmed as characters to do, and as people to like to see. But now things did not seem to be like this. It was as if Verity and I, each by risking something extreme – myself by going off to see Rosemary; Verity by seeming to ac-cept this (or whatever else she might have been up to while I was away) – had perhaps called the bluff of our knee-jerk cycle of resentment and complaint, and had achieved some other style of resolution. Verity did not ask about my time in America. I did not go back over the traumas attendant on the publication of my book. I went back to writing the second volume about my father, which dealt with the time when, with my mother now dead, my father lived with and then married Diana. Verity had not got on well with Diana; she had thought her a racist. There would surely be no need for Verity and me to be in contention over this part of my writing.

- 24 -

I said earlier that I had wished Verity could play a part in writing at least the last chapters of this book. One of the points of my *Catastrophe Practice* books and of *Impossible Object* before them, was the idea that to get at truth – just as to get at the understanding of a character – there has to be the recognition that truth and understanding are multifaceted; they cannot be pinned down; they need to be seen in two or more ways at once; and then by this, as it were, they may be able to sort themselves out. And part of this process is the necessity to acknowledge bad times as well as good; not simply because one can learn from one's mistakes, but because evolution itself depends on mistakes – the old has to be sloughed off before something new can emerge. But battles still have to be fought against what seems bad; and in battle good is often endangered too. Nothing here is clear-cut, straightforward: things have to be risked, in the hope that something worthwhile may develop. Or if it does not, then something at least may have been learnt.

And then it seemed that risk, learning, are essentially personal. If a relationship is to change, then truth and salvation still have to be looked for and found in the individual mind and heart. This is in the domain of what as it were goes on off stage; and it is then that a change in relationship will either become manifest, or it may not.

Verity and I settled back in the studio-cottages, with the big house once more let. Our life in Majorca enjoyed an Indian summer with our grand new swimming-pool, the beach having become somewhat crowded. I was now earning money not just from books but from film options and scripts, though *The Assassination of Trotsky* and *Impossible Object* were the only films that were made. (Experienced script-writers advise that this is the least troublesome way to make money.) Verity went back into analysis and group analysis; later we went together to marital therapy. All this turned out well, so that Verity was soon training to be a psychotherapist herself. She did this with an organisation called Arbours, which runs houses for people too disturbed to be all right on their own but not serious enough to be detained legally. And before long Verity was practising successfully as a psychotherapist, working both with her own patients and with groups in hospitals – these mostly caring for young people clinically depressed or with eating disorders. She has recently (2005) withdrawn from hospital work because she found herself out of step with its current emphasis on set procedures and targets, but she continues to exercise her more personal skills with patients who come to her at home. She also teaches – in seminars with students at her old training ground of Arbours. Verity's story is specifically one of using experience of her old 'hard times' to initiate good times for herself and others.

My own hard times now followed a pattern by which, when it seemed I was on the brink of behaving obnoxiously, I would happen to fall and break a leg. Since my original debilitating car crash I have fallen and broken again first one femur and then the other, and have had both hip and knee replacements. So that then not only do I become dependent on Verity for help, but it is not so easy to practise my old means of survival when things became difficult by running away. But I nevertheless found once more a two-room flat near Church Row to which I could retreat in order to work.

But then when the time came for me to have my hip replacement it so happened that Verity and I were becoming once more locked in battle. I can't remember why: nowadays this kind of thing seems so silly; it was as if malignant characters from soap operas had once more come back to possess us. I had thought we had learnt to handle this sort of thing by recognising that although this perhaps inevitably happened to 'on-stage' humanity, there was always the off-stage reality which might be trusted. So to recuperate after the hip operation I went to a religiously orientated convalescent home where there was a daily Mass and laying-on of hands. But here it seemed that I had a regression to a primitive desire that life should be all-of-a-piece and faultless. I wrote to Verity to complain that I thought that we should surely not be behaving in the old way now since when I got out of convalescence I would still need to recuperate, and as things were it did not seem that I would return to a healing home. I soon realised that this reversion to recrimination was a miserable mistake – unless it might be in the style of Mephistopheles, doing bad on the unconscious chance of engendering good. Anyway, I had a furious reply from Verity saying that she had thought indeed that we had got beyond this nonsense, and rejecting my dismal complaint. And then when I was driven back by a man-friend to my flat where I worked, I found not only a notice from the landlords saying that my floor had dry-rot and would have to be taken up, but a letter from Verity's solicitor saying that since I did not wish to return to her 'not-heal-ing' home, she was initiating proceedings for formal separation.

– Oh the horror!

– Oh the inevitability.

– But there was some new direction here! No apologies or whinging or nagging –

But how would I have once hoped to handle this?

Before my operation I had been about to embark on the last book of the *Catastrophe Practice* series, *Hopeful Monsters*, which was about the two eldest of the actors on and off stage. They had met and become lovers in the nineteen thirties; they had lived together, gone apart, come together again and married; gone off, remained closely in touch. They had each felt they had work to do separately; they had seen their life together as a pulse, a heart-beat. In their middle- and old-age, which occurs in the time-scale of the previous books, they find themselves offering to others chances to learn what they have learned about the paradoxes of life – one as a professor and the other as a psychoanalyst. Their pupils are those of a younger generation who turn up in their path – the protagonists of *Imago Bird, Serpent, Judith.*

In order to do research for the early years of the couple in *Hopeful Monsters* I had planned to spend some time in the north-east of England learning about conditions there in the industrial slump of the 1930s when my then young man, Max, had gone there to do good works. I was now still walking with two sticks; and I thought this semblance of an old man returning to scenes of youth might give some verisimilitude to what I would be finding. I did nothing about Verity's lawyer's letter except to let my own lawyer know.

I had a friend who lived in an old back-to-back house in an ex-mining village near Durham. I went to stay with her, and from there explored the environment and the libraries. I learned that it was on this coast that Christianity had first come to Britain, brought by saints in cockleshell boats risking their lives in rough seas. Centuries later, in the impoverished nineteen thirties, I learned that one of the most popular games that children played consisted of squeezing themselves in a foetus position within a rubber tyre, and then getting themselves rolled helplessly and dangerously down a steep slope. 'Hopeful monsters' was a phrase coined by a biologist in the 1940s to describe the major mutations that might, very rarely, take over from current species if it chanced that their risky style was more suited to a changed environment. The most likely chance was that they would be snuffed out.

From Durham I went on to Holy Island, where it was very cold. I found a bed-and-breakfast place and sat wrapped up in bed with my typewriter on my knee. I thought of those old hopeful monsters in their cockleshell boats; the children who found that in games that risked everything an impoverished life might be made to seem worthwhile; and I wondered how in God's name I might imagine myself a hopeful monster, propped up alone once more with my crutches in a freezing b-and-b place on Holy Island. In my story my hero Max, a scientist, looks out across the North Sea to where two real-life physicists from Germany, refugees from Nazism, were sharing a vision of how a controlled splitting of an atom might be possible. Things that were joined together might fly violently apart; but from this there could, or might not, come about new configurations.

When I got back to London I found that the floor of one of the two rooms of my flat was still removed, but I could settle in the other. I was excited by what I had come across in the north; so I disconnected the telephone and settled down to work. Might not new configurations be available in the mind?

I was getting along quite well when one day there was a knock on the door. But no one should know I was here! When I opened the door I found Verity in the passage with a policeman. I thought – My God, she has come to arrest me! She looked somewhat anxious. She said 'I thought you might be dead.' I said 'Well I'm not.' She said 'I tried to ring you, and to come round, but I couldn't get through or in.' I thought – So perhaps after all we are hopeful monsters! The policeman said 'Then

you're all right?' I said 'Yes.' Verity said 'I've brought you some food.'
I said 'That's terribly kind.' The policeman said 'Well I can be getting
along then.'

I am telling this story here somewhat trimmed and tidied because
a lot of irrelevant 'business' necessarily goes on on-stage; and this is
a story about what must have been going on off-stage. This can never
precisely be known; or rather known only through what occurs on
stage being apprehended as an impossible object or art-work. Such is a
God's-eye view; God himself being off-stage. But God comes on-stage
in the character, surely, of some loved-one exemplifying the goodness
of the human heart.

*

I do not know how much more there need be of this story. The writing begins to slip, loses grip, becomes boring. The prospect of peace at
last?

Verity and I were back together once more; it was again difficult to
remember just why we had been apart. It was just before this time, I
think, that Verity had taken her chances to go off – to Cornwall, to
Switzerland – with a charismatic friend or lover of whom I had become aware – but so what, had not this seemed a not unreasonable way
of dealing with our predicaments? There seemed to have been other
friends or would-be lovers. Once when our cottages were being repaired
and I was in my flat, Verity and the children retired to a grand house
full of antiques in Pimlico which had been lent to her. She seemed to
manage her excursions more pragmatically than I: and for this should
I not be grateful? When Freddie Ayer, the well-known philosopher and
philanderer, found himself at a dinner party sitting next to Verity, and

was bemoaning to her about how in his old age he was fed up with life and would do away with himself if he only knew how, Verity did her trademark flirt-act with him – 'I've never heard such rubbish in all my life!' and gave him instructions about how many paracetamols to take. Freddie took out his notebook to write this down, and people at the dinner party imagined he was taking down her telephone number – which doubtless he also was. And then for the rest of his life he would frequently ring up Verity for a consoling or encouraging chat. Well this was the style of hopeful monsters, was it not?

I came at last to the end of *Hopeful Monsters,* and thus of the whole *Catastrophe Practice* series. The previous novels had got respectful reviews though no one had yet dealt comprehensively with the whole concept. Then in 1990 *Hopeful Monsters* won the Whitbread Book of the Year award, and at the presentation ceremony Verity's pleasure was so evident that she seemed to have forgiven my years of self-obsession.

With *Can Rave* now during some holidays being profitably let, we began to take the chance to travel with the children – to Venice, to China, to Kenya on safari. Verity and I travelled round much of India – over the Himalayas to Ladakh, down to Madurai in the south – then on to Laos and Cambodia. These times of travel were free of conflict like the holidays in *Can Rave* and *Cala Senau* had for the most part been: there was too much to watch and wonder at in the outside world for the paradoxes of consciousness to invade.

Eventually, when the children had grown up and I was growing old, we sold *Can Rave*, and handed over *Cala Senau* and its by now rather comfortable boathouse to our son Marius. Verity and I still sometimes go there; when I swim I leave my crutches or sticks on the rocks and Marius and Jonathan circle round me as if protecting me from sharks.

Before this there had been the necessity to consider how Verity and I and the children were to settle all together in London. I had kept my flat to work in which was a few minutes walk from Church Row; but this ludicrously extravagant life-style could no longer be funded by juggling the lettings of the big house and cottages. And anyway, with it now seeming increasingly unlikely that our marriage would ever decisively break, it should surely be possible to give the on-stage appearance of a sensible family. But to do this it seemed clear that we should sell not only my flat, but the house in Church Row and the studio-cottages. The former was too inconvenient and grand, and the others too tumble-down and constricting. And the property market was now booming.

I was due to go on a trip to America to stay with my American publisher, John O'Brien, who was embarking on publishing *Catastrophe Practice* for his Dalkey Archive Press. Verity said she would look for a house for us in Kilburn or Kentish Town where properties were cheaper; and only as a last resort for a room next door where I could work if it was still felt that my permanent presence would send us mad. (But had it not been my toing-and-froing that had sent us mad?) (Or kept us sane?)

John O'Brien lived in the quiet outskirts of Chicago. In the mornings I would work on the *Catastrophe Practice* plays trying to make what they were 'up to' more explicit. (Well what *is* going on off stage?) In the afternoons I would walk in the surprisingly beautiful nearby woods and ruminate – how can things be made explicit that everyone has to learn for themselves? In the evenings I would talk with John. He would say – Nicholas, however much you tinker with those plays, you will never turn them into something that people won't have to work at to understand. But that's what you want, isn't it?

Verity telephoned from London to say that she had looked at several houses, but the only one that had seemed any good – in fact had seemed perfect – was one between Camden Town and Regent's Park, but this was considerably more expensive than the sort of figure we had talked about. So if we wanted it we would have to pool all our resources, and there could be no more nonsense, or luxury, of trying (and failing) to get the best of separate worlds. In the Camden Town house however there was a basement in which it would be perfect for me to work; it even had its own bathroom and kitchen; so we might (good heavens!) even get the best of the same world. But a decision had to be made quickly. I said – Make an offer, and keep things going till I get back. I wondered – This might be the sort of place where parallel lines meet?

So I flew home, and went to see this house, and it seemed obvious that we should buy it. The Church Row house had already been sold, and now Verity set about getting the best price for the studio-cottages. This she did; and this seemed to make up for all our previous extravagance. And now the freehold of the new house could be in Verity's name; so that I would be freed from some of the temptations and corruptions of power.

For a time we all camped in this basement while the house upstairs was being repaired. I found I was hardly missing my once so much loved Hampstead homes – in which there had been so many remarkable and traumatic dramas and performances. In the new house drama would doubtless continue, but with luck more in the style of a theatre-in-the-round in which there can be more realistic and ironic connections between actors and audience.

And this is where we are some eighteen years later.

So beyond this, what more indeed is there to be said?

The children are perhaps the real heroes of this story – Marius and Jonathan and my four with Rosemary – Shaun and Ivo and Robert and Clare. With parents and step-parents so often demented they have learned – what – how not to be like them? There has usually been the honesty all round to make this just possible – honesty about the bad things as well as the good, and the trying to move on from the former, which has been the theme of this book. It strikes me as I near the end that there has not been enough in it about the good times; and writers (and God knows most humans) usually have this problem – bad things are dramatic and thus more easy to hold in mind and describe. But I have tried to put the 'good' into my novels as well as here – the way in which things can work out truly in spite of what has been bad – and if people say they cannot see what I am 'up to,' then so what. They can see, if they wish, Verity's and my children, and the way they now look after their own children and even their elderly parents – so some things, yes, work out for the good in spite of the bad.

Verity has become, as I have said, a matriarchal figure to my and Rosemary's children. Rosemary herself, when she was back in the Isle of Man, was grateful for this. After the operation on her back she even planned to get a part-time flat by Regent's Park, which is near where Verity and I live. I glimpsed a fulfilment of my dream of an as it were infinitely extended family, in which everyone had learned to try to be kind to everyone else.

And then, in the Isle of Man, Rosemary suddenly and unexpectedly had a stroke. She was found by her cleaning-lady unconscious.

Her children and I flew up to the Isle of Man. We sat round her bedside in the hospital while she remained unconscious. During these last years she had been painting strangely evocative pictures – one series on the story of Little Red Riding Hood and the Wolf; another on Alice in Wonderland. These were in contrast to the alarming watercolours of a disintegrating urban society she had been doing while propped up on the waterfront of Los Angeles. Little Red Riding Hood runs eagerly across an open landscape with a basket of food for her grandmother; then in a forest of thick stems and leaves she comes face to face with the wolf. They stand still, confronting one another. Then in the last picture of the series Little Red Riding Hood is gobbled up in a whirl like that of a hurricane.

Rosemary never regained consciousness. There came a time when the doctors told the children and me that she was now technically brain-dead, and they asked us – did we agree that the machine that was keeping her artificially breathing should be switched off? This seemed a question impossible to answer. After a time the machine was switched off.

Verity came up for the funeral and many of Rosemary's relations and friends. There seemed no one to organise the gathering afterwards, so Verity took this on and the party went well.

Later, in London, in place of a memorial service, the children organised a large exhibition of Rosemary's paintings – the kind of exhibition that she had seldom been interested in arranging herself. There were the early Sussex seascapes and landscapes; the horses by the sea in Languedoc; the intimations of urban life collapsing in America, and the solitary girl confronting at least for a moment a respectful wolf. After the exhibition most of the paintings were due to go on show in the Isle of Man. They were being stored there in a warehouse until the gallery was free to hang them, and one night the warehouse caught fire and everything in it was destroyed. This seemed to me an almost unimaginable disaster. But the best of the early seascapes and three of the Little Red Riding Hood paintings had been kept by the family, and were saved.

I grieve for Rosemary. I should have done more to help her deal with her pursuing wolf.

*

I had thought that *Paradoxes of Peace* might be an argument for the existence of God – on the grounds that the demands made on humans by life are naturally paradoxical, and humans fall inevitably into war unless some experience of the supernatural holds paradoxes at peace. God is thus a hypothesis that can in some sense be put to the test; though the results will not be able to be assessed validly by anyone except oneself.

People have evolved religious stories to illustrate patterns of how things happen religiously. I have hoped that this book may be seen as a religious story. Not a moral story, no. Nor one that quite makes sense.

I do not nowadays often go to church. I go at Christmas and Easter, with Verity and whoever of the family happen to be with us. It is like visiting a venerable and much loved parent who is somewhat disabled. On the way this may be seen as a bit of a duty; but then – how blessed that one should still find oneself able to be dutiful! The Church is the holder of the story, the secrets.

For years I did not visit the House of the Resurrection at Mirfield; I had moved in a different way. The Community's reaction to my book about Father Raynes had been paradoxical: brethren had praised it, but did not wish to have it on show. Then Verity and I went to Mirfield to attend my old friend Aelred's funeral; and for me this was like visiting a childhood home. Steve Biko's widow and his son flew from South Africa to be there; and with them Verity felt at home.

Verity and I have kept together, and alive; and it does not seem possible to think of being parted except by death. She looks after me, as I have said, beautifully, in the disablement of my old age. I do not nowadays venture far from the house without her and my wheelchair. There are occasional rows and angers, but it was when I used to become unpleasant that I tended to fall and break a leg. And then Verity and I naturally, as I have said, got on better again. The last time I broke a leg this was the one which had already had the hip replacement, so the metal replacement had to be replaced and I landed up with one leg three inches shorter than the other. So that now when I do manage to walk I roll like a ship in a high wind.

Verity said – You punish yourself!

I said – I remember thinking that it can be proper to be punished, so that one is then freed to make jokes.

But nowadays it seems better to make jokes and not break a leg.

The Christian images that I like to keep in mind are those whimsical smiling figures in early Armenian or Coptic churches who do not seem interested in images of the crucifixion or of judgement, but rather in the joyful oddity of what came after the resurrection.

However one of the last times I got home from hospital and was still on crutches I began to feel as if I were being chivvied again as in the old days by the hounds of heaven or hell. For years I had not felt the need to make a formal confession: I now found myself asking Verity to drive me to my old spiritual knocking-shop of All Saints, Margaret Street. She said – Why, what have you done? I said – Perhaps it's because I have done nothing. Verity, now a wise psychotherapist, drove me there. I said – I can find my own way home.

All Saints Margaret Street had not changed. It was like an exquisite railway station with people waiting for their last train to come in. I thought – But thank goodness I have had time to see a bit of the Holy City! When my turn came I got on my knees as it were on the edge of a platform looking down at the rails. I thought – One push and I am over. People had told me I must not break my leg again.

I said to the unknown priest – 'I don't quite know why I'm here, except that I haven't been to confession for thirty years.' He said 'Well I think it's extraordinarily good of you to come now!' I said – just the ordinary rubbishy things: obsessive selfishness, lack of care for those closest to me, lack of love. He said 'Tell me your Christian name and I will pray for you.' I said 'That's extraordinarily kind!'

One should not hang around too long for one's train to come in.

I am in my mid eighties. I still do not know how to think about death. The problem for humans is surely not what happens after death, but how to endure the staying alive. In my seventies I was diagnosed with leukaemia and the chemotherapy almost killed me: I shook so much that my bed seemed in runaway to hell. There is a comic film in which a coffin on a bier on wheels escapes down a hill with its mourners running after it. I said to myself then that if I recovered I would take my shotgun to Regent's Park and shoot myself in order never to be aware of being so helpless again. But then I had what it seemed might be called a near-death experience: from the ceiling I looked down on myself laid out naked and rather beautiful on my bed in the shape of a broken-limbed cross.

It seems to me now that Verity and I have got so often under one another's skin that we must indeed, for ill or good, have become what is meant by one flesh. When one of us is suicidal then the other is likely to be suicidal too; so indeed what is the point of breaking a leg? There's not even nowadays much of a stumbling-block about the Trinity –

What?

One substance, three persons: you know? The triple-whammy paradox. Two people don't seem to be able to be at peace without the presence of – but one shouldn't talk much about the Holy Spirit, the Spirit of truth, the Comforter.

Will you please shut up?

Willingly. I have subtitled this book *The Presence of Infinity* – infinity being that which, like the unseen matter of the universe, goes on so wondrously off-stage.

But death goes on on-stage.

To be sure. And how we love being told about it!

So what's wrong with oblivion?

Nothing. Just better perhaps to have done a bit to be comforted about first.

Post Script 2008

For Easter Weekend 2008, some two years after I finished this book, my children arranged a family get-together in a beautiful barn-like building adapted for such occasions in Gloucestershire – Verity and I, children, grandchildren, wives and girlfriends, some thirty in all – and we had two days and two nights which were amazingly happy – so this was a gift of more than comfort, yes.

SELECTED DALKEY ARCHIVE PAPERBACKS

FOR A FULL LIST OF PUBLICATIONS, VISIT:
www.dalkeyarchive.com

SELECTED DALKEY ARCHIVE PAPERBACKS

HARRY MATHEWS,
    The Case of the Persevering Maltese: Collected Essays.
    Cigarettes.
    The Conversions.
    The Human Country: New and Collected Stories.
    The Journalist.
    My Life in CIA.
    Singular Pleasures.
    The Sinking of the Odradek Stadium.
    Tlooth.
    20 Lines a Day.
ROBERT L. McLAUGHLIN, ED.,
    Innovations: An Anthology of Modern &
      Contemporary Fiction.
HERMAN MELVILLE, *The Confidence-Man.*
AMANDA MICHALOPOULOU, *I'd Like.*
STEVEN MILLHAUSER, *The Barnum Museum.*
    In the Penny Arcade.
RALPH J. MILLS, JR., *Essays on Poetry.*
OLIVE MOORE, *Spleen.*
NICHOLAS MOSLEY, *Accident.*
    Assassins.
    Catastrophe Practice.
    Children of Darkness and Light.
    Experience and Religion.
    God's Hazard.
    The Hesperides Tree.
    Hopeful Monsters.
    Imago Bird.
    Impossible Object.
    Inventing God.
    Judith.
    Look at the Dark.
    Natalie Natalia.
    Paradoxes of Peace.
    Serpent.
    Time at War.
    The Uses of Slime Mould: Essays of Four Decades.
WARREN MOTTE,
    Fables of the Novel: French Fiction since 1990.
    Fiction Now: The French Novel in the 21st Century.
    Oulipo: A Primer of Potential Literature.
YVES NAVARRE, *Our Share of Time.*
    Sweet Tooth.
DOROTHY NELSON, *In Night's City.*
    Tar and Feathers.
WILFRIDO D. NOLLEDO, *But for the Lovers.*
FLANN O'BRIEN, *At Swim-Two-Birds.*
    At War.
    The Best of Myles.
    The Dalkey Archive.
    Further Cuttings.
    The Hard Life.
    The Poor Mouth.
    The Third Policeman.
CLAUDE OLLIER, *The Mise-en-Scène.*
PATRIK OUŘEDNÍK, *Europeana.*
FERNANDO DEL PASO, *News from the Empire.*
    Palinuro of Mexico.
ROBERT PINGET, *The Inquisitory.*
    Mahu or The Material.
    Trio.
MANUEL PUIG, *Betrayed by Rita Hayworth.*
RAYMOND QUENEAU, *The Last Days.*
    Odile.
    Pierrot Mon Ami.
    Saint Glinglin.
ANN QUIN, *Berg.*
    Passages.
    Three.
    Tripticks.
ISHMAEL REED, *The Free-Lance Pallbearers.*
    The Last Days of Louisiana Red.
    Reckless Eyeballing.
    The Terrible Threes.
    The Terrible Twos.
    Yellow Back Radio Broke-Down.
JEAN RICARDOU, *Place Names.*
RAINER MARIA RILKE,
    The Notebooks of Malte Laurids Brigge.
JULIÁN RÍOS, *Larva: A Midsummer Night's Babel.*
    Poundemonium.
AUGUSTO ROA BASTOS, *I the Supreme.*
OLIVIER ROLIN, *Hotel Crystal.*
JACQUES ROUBAUD, *The Form of a City Changes Faster,*
    Alas, Than the Human Heart.
    The Great Fire of London.
    Hortense in Exile.
    Hortense Is Abducted.
    The Loop.
    The Plurality of Worlds of Lewis.
    The Princess Hoppy.
    Some Thing Black.
LEON S. ROUDIEZ, *French Fiction Revisited.*

VEDRANA RUDAN, *Night.*
LYDIE SALVAYRE, *The Company of Ghosts.*
    Everyday Life.
    The Lecture.
    The Power of Flies.
LUIS RAFAEL SÁNCHEZ, *Macho Camacho's Beat.*
SEVERO SARDUY, *Cobra & Maitreya.*
NATHALIE SARRAUTE, *Do You Hear Them?*
    Martereau.
    The Planetarium.
ARNO SCHMIDT, *Collected Stories.*
    Nobodaddy's Children.
CHRISTINE SCHUTT, *Nightwork.*
GAIL SCOTT, *My Paris.*
DAMION SEARLS, *What We Were Doing and Where We*
    Were Going.
JUNE AKERS SEESE,
    Is This What Other Women Feel Too?
    What Waiting Really Means.
BERNARD SHARE, *Inish.*
    Transit.
AURELIE SHEEHAN, *Jack Kerouac Is Pregnant.*
VIKTOR SHKLOVSKY, *Knight's Move.*
    A Sentimental Journey: Memoirs 1917–1922.
    Energy of Delusion: A Book on Plot.
    Literature and Cinematography.
    Theory of Prose.
    Third Factory.
    Zoo, or Letters Not about Love.
JOSEF ŠKVORECKÝ,
    The Engineer of Human Souls.
CLAUDE SIMON, *The Invitation.*
GILBERT SORRENTINO, *Aberration of Starlight.*
    Blue Pastoral.
    Crystal Vision.
    Imaginative Qualities of Actual Things.
    Mulligan Stew.
    Pack of Lies.
    Red the Fiend.
    The Sky Changes.
    Something Said.
    Splendide-Hôtel.
    Steelwork.
    Under the Shadow.
W. M. SPACKMAN, *The Complete Fiction.*
GERTRUDE STEIN, *Lucy Church Amiably.*
    The Making of Americans.
    A Novel of Thank You.
PIOTR SZEWC, *Annihilation.*
STEFAN THEMERSON, *Hobson's Island.*
    The Mystery of the Sardine.
    Tom Harris.
JEAN-PHILIPPE TOUSSAINT, *The Bathroom.*
    Camera.
    Monsieur.
    Television.
DUMITRU TSEPENEAG, *Pigeon Post.*
    The Necessary Marriage.
    Vain Art of the Fugue.
ESTHER TUSQUETS, *Stranded.*
DUBRAVKA UGRESIC, *Lend Me Your Character.*
    Thank You for Not Reading.
MATI UNT, *Brecht at Night*
    Diary of a Blood Donor.
    Things in the Night.
ÁLVARO URIBE AND OLIVIA SEARS, EDS.,
    The Best of Contemporary Mexican Fiction.
ELOY URROZ, *The Obstacles.*
LUISA VALENZUELA, *He Who Searches.*
PAUL VERHAEGHEN, *Omega Minor.*
MARJA-LIISA VARTIO, *The Parson's Widow.*
BORIS VIAN, *Heartsnatcher.*
AUSTRYN WAINHOUSE, *Hedyphagetica.*
PAUL WEST, *Words for a Deaf Daughter & Gala.*
CURTIS WHITE, *America's Magic Mountain.*
    The Idea of Home.
    Memories of My Father Watching TV.
    Monstrous Possibility: An Invitation to
      Literary Politics.
    Requiem.
DIANE WILLIAMS, *Excitability: Selected Stories.*
    Romancer Erector.
DOUGLAS WOOLF, *Wall to Wall.*
    Ya! & John-Juan.
JAY WRIGHT, *Polynomials and Pollen.*
    The Presentable Art of Reading Absence.
PHILIP WYLIE, *Generation of Vipers.*
MARGUERITE YOUNG, *Angel in the Forest.*
    Miss MacIntosh, My Darling.
REYOUNG, *Unbabbling.*
ZORAN ŽIVKOVIĆ, *Hidden Camera.*
LOUIS ZUKOFSKY, *Collected Fiction.*
SCOTT ZWIREN, *God Head.*

FOR A FULL LIST OF PUBLICATIONS, VISIT:
www.dalkeyarchive.com